Best Hikes With
CHILDREN®

in New Mexico

By Bob Julyan

THE
MOUNTAINEERS

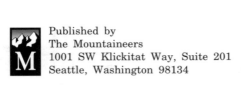
Published by
The Mountaineers
1001 SW Klickitat Way, Suite 201
Seattle, Washington 98134

Published simultaneously in Great Britain by Cordee, 3a DeMontfort
Street, Leicester, England, LE1 7HD

First printing 1994, second printing 1996, revised 2001

Manufactured in the United States of America

Edited by Ramona Gault
Maps by Amy Budge
All photographs by the author except as noted
Book layout by Richard Carter
Typesetting by The Mountaineers Books

Cover photograph: *The Bisti Wilderness Area, hike 41 (Photo: Dan Peha)*
Title page: *A mountain pond in the Sangre de Cristo Mountains near Palo
Flechado Pass*

Library of Congress Cataloging-in-Publication Data
Julyan, Bob.
    Best hikes with children in New Mexico / by Bob Julyan.
        p.   cm.
    Includes index.
    ISBN 0-89886-370-8
    1. Hiking—New Mexico—Guidebooks. 2. Outdoor recreation for
children—New Mexico—Guidebooks. 3. New Mexico Guidebooks.
I. Title.
GV199.42.N62J85   1994
796.5'1'09789—dc20   94-7434
                                                            CIP

*This book is dedicated to the memory of
Conard, Chub, and Kenny,
who gave me the mountains,
and to my family,
especially Robyn, and her friends
Jessica, Holly, and Amanda*

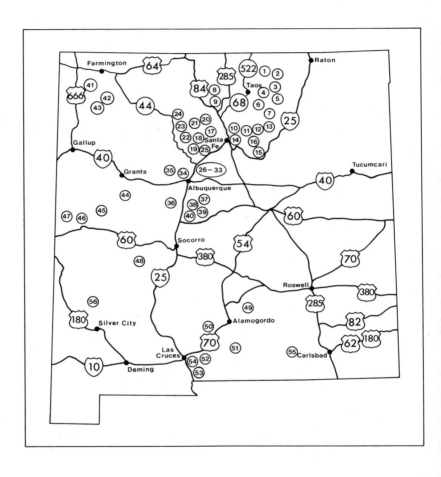

Contents

Introduction

The desert east of Socorro was parched and harsh, filled with cacti and creosote bush the day my wife, Mary, and I hiked there with our daughter Megan, then four. We had driven down from Albuquerque to explore the Upper Sonoran life zone, and we had picked a site to park our old camper van almost at random in the maze of dry washes and nameless hills. No national park ever would be established here, my wife and I commented, but we were having a good time nonetheless—hiking in the clear desert air, warmed by the bright New Mexico sun, the three of us together, discovering all sorts of unexpected beauty in the wilderness. Still, I wondered, what of our daughter? What was here for her? Was it fair to drag her along on our eccentric adventures?

Suddenly I stopped, for at my feet I noticed the skeleton of a desert millipede, its 5-inch segmented carapace bleached white by the intense sun. Carefully, I picked it up and said, "Here, Megan, look at this," as I held it out to her. Her eyes grew wide with wonder as she stretched out her two tiny palms to receive my gift. "Oh, Dad!" she said with utmost sincerity. "*Thank you* for this dead millipede."

Such are the joys of hiking with children. And another act of faith rewarded.

We parents live on the faith that the things we've found to be beautiful and true in our lives also will prove so for our children. That's why we hikers hike with our children.

My wife and I had decided that hiking was something good the family did, that it bound us together in positive ways, and that because our two daughters are part of the family, they, too, are hikers, at least while they're in our care. Just as we have a right and a responsibility to insist that they eat balanced and healthy meals, so we also may insist that they live balanced and healthy lives. For us, that includes hiking.

But taking our children hiking not only is good for them but also is good for us. Much as I enjoy hikes by myself or with other adults, I must admit that hikes with my children have more humor, more fantasy, more adventures, more life. Small things in nature, such as seeing a tarantula or finding animal bones, are magnified when seen through children's eyes. When I hike with my children, I'm often reminded of the phrase "You're never too old to have a happy childhood."

I don't know yet whether my children will absorb from our hikes a love of nature and a love of outdoor recreation. Again, that's an act of faith. But I do know they will carry with them into adulthood memories of good family times—from roasted marshmallows to humorous encounters with skunks. And that really should be all we expect from our family hikes.

The most precious three words a child can utter to a parent at the end of a hike, after "I love you," are "That was fun."

Using This Book

Children's and adults' interests don't necessarily coincide, and in choosing hikes with children adults need to consider what appeals to kids. This shouldn't be too difficult—after all, we were kids ourselves at one time—but perhaps we need to remind ourselves of what specifically will appeal to children on a particular hike. I've included trips that appeal to both children and adults. For the children, I've tried to ensure that each trip features something of interest besides scenery. Nothing against scenery, but whenever I've asked my children what they recall about hikes, they always seem to remember the waterfall slide or the tadpole pond or the mysterious cave or the weird-shaped climbing rocks more than the play of sunlight on the hillside. For the adults, I've chosen routes that will be interesting and appealing for them as well.

For example, on the Bisti hike adults may appreciate the geological significance of the area, but children are more likely to remember the petrified logs they encounter. At Tsankawi Ruins, adults will ponder the lifestyle of the Indians who once lived on the Pajarito Plateau, but children will be more interested in exploring the caves where the Indians lived. Both adults and children will love playing on the dunes of White Sands National Monument, just as both should enjoy looking for the ancient Indian carvings at Piedras Marcadas Canyon in Petroglyph National Monument.

The 56 hikes are grouped according to regions of the state, as indicated by the map on page 4. Each numbered hike includes 1) an information block, which gives a summary of important facts about the hike; 2) symbols for features of special interest; 3) a map; and 4) a description of the hike.

The information blocks state whether the hike is a dayhike or an overnight trip. Most of the hikes can be completed in one day or less, but camping opportunities are noted, and a few hikes are primarily overnight excursions.

In the information block, each hike is rated as easy, moderate, or difficult for children, based on such criteria as distance, elevation gain, and trail conditions. For example, a hike listed as easy should be within the abilities of very young children. But these ratings are relative and subjective, and individual children vary widely in their stamina and energy, even from day to day. If you're uncertain about

Hikers descending an arroyo in Embudo Canyon, with the cliffs of the Sandia Mountains in the distance

your child's limits, start easy. It's much better for a child to finish a hike exulting that it was too easy than complaining it was too hard.

The information block for each hike also lists which months are most appropriate for the hike. That varies widely in New Mexico. For example, November can bring shirt-sleeve weather—or a blizzard. The months indicated are only general guidelines. Each information block includes an estimate of the one-way distance for the complete hike, the starting and ending elevations, a list of appropriate supplemental maps, and a statement of any hazards for children that are unique to the hike.

Where appropriate, each hike description also points out turn-arounds—convenient and scenic places to end the hike and still feel satisfied. Because of these, don't restrict your search for easy or moderate hikes only to those labeled such, because more difficult hikes with turnarounds might also be suitable.

Similarly, be flexible in using the information about when the trip is hikable. I've tried to indicate the optimum months for each hike, but in New Mexico day-to-day conditions can vary widely, especially in the winter. My family and I frequently hike in shirt sleeves in

January. In the summer, a hike that would be intolerable under the midday sun can be a delight in the early morning or late evening.

At the beginning of this book is a table of contents map showing where the hikes are distributed throughout New Mexico. Along with each hike description is a map showing parking areas, the trail, and other information specific to that hike. These maps are only for general reference, however, and other maps should be taken as well.

To help with this, I have listed with each trip description the name of the U.S. Geological Survey (USGS) 7.5-minute quadrangle covering the hike. Although often lacking current trail and road numbers, these maps still are the most detailed and useful for orienting yourself in the landscape, as they show elevation and topographical relief. Where appropriate, the name of the U.S. Forest Service or national or state park map also is listed for each hike; though they often don't show relief, their road and trail information generally is more current.

Trail distances expressed in decimals imply more precision than is actually feasible. Still, all measurements are as accurate as possible.

Keeping Children Happy

As every parent knows, on family trips it's hard for anyone to be happy unless everyone is happy. And when hiking with children that means planning, patience, psychology, and, very often, out-and-out chicanery and bribery. Here are some techniques of proven effectiveness:

Include children in decisions and planning. While the ultimate responsibility for trip planning and preparation rests with adults, the more the children are involved, the greater their stake in the trip's success. What does the child think should be essential equipment for the hike? Who should carry it? What should be in each person's pack? What food or snacks should be taken? When should the party take a break? All these and more are decisions that give children a sense of participating in the hike rather than merely being taken along.

Choose the right hike for your family. Knowing your child's abilities and signals on the trail requires experience. For example, children, especially young ones, often begin a hike with a surge of bounding, youthful enthusiasm that they cannot sustain and that soon leaves them exhausted. In this situation it's up to the adults to set a more realistic pace. Also, children can go from eager energy to collapsed exhaustion with surprising rapidity; try to learn your child's signals of approaching fatigue.

And parents need to consider distance from a child's perspective. From my childhood in Colorado's Front Range I remember 3-mile hikes that to me seemed like Himalayan treks. Sometimes a half-mile is all a child has the energy or the attention for. I recall doing the Peñasco Blanco Ruins hike 42 when our oldest daughter was three; it was only 2 miles on mostly level ground—easily within her abilities—but it took 2 hours because she had to investigate every bug that crossed our path. And sometimes a 2-mile hike becomes a half-mile hike if the child discovers a great place to explore or a pond for skipping stones. Flexibility is the key to successful hiking with children.

Let them know what to expect. One of the most common mistakes adults make in hiking with children is being vague and misleading about the length or difficulty of the trip. Just as in a long car trip, a frequent and legitimate question is "When are we going to get there?" The more definite and realistic your answers, the more readily children will accept what you ask of them. An excellent technique is to teach children some map-reading skills, or better yet, let the child be the official map-reader for the trip.

Give a pre-hike talk. Before beginning a hike, it doesn't hurt to remind children—positively but firmly—of the realities of nature, such as the possible presence of hazards like poison ivy or flash flooding, and the rules of the trail, such as the party not separating, as well as any appropriate family regulations, like no bickering.

Let the child take a friend along. Not only does the presence of a friend encourage good behavior and motivation, but also children are less inclined to become bored and to nag if a buddy is along. And this relieves you of the burden of providing entertainment and conversation.

Let the child lead. Children hike faster and become more involved in the hike when they're in the lead. Throw in a little sibling rivalry, and you've got it made. But make sure the rotations are regular and fair; change leaders at prearranged times or points. And don't hesitate to insist on an appropriate pace or on leading yourself when conditions warrant it.

Pack trail treats. It will be a dark day for the candy companies when my children finally outgrow trail treats. Prudently rationed, judiciously doled out, trail treats have a way of compensating for steep hills and trails that seem never to end.

Take frequent breaks. Recognize that times and distances that seem short to adults can seem long and tedious to children. Sometimes it's difficult to assess children's fatigue. A good rule of thumb is the following: When in doubt, break. Keep breaks brief, however, lest children lose the momentum of hiking. And especially in New Mexico, use breaks as an opportunity to keep your children well hydrated—with water, not sugar fluids. Also remember that if you wait until you're thirsty to drink, you've waited too long.

Use stories, games, and playfulness. When the going really gets tough, I tell stories to my kids. Children have a wonderfully ingenuous capacity to ignore their discomforts when engrossed in a tale. What's more, they'll usually listen as long as you're willing to talk.

Games also are effective in keeping children happy and moving. Counting wildflower species, with appropriate treats as rewards. Looking for colors in nature that match those worn by children. Fantasies about boulder trolls or tree squeaks. Whatever. One of the greatest rewards of having children is being allowed to share some of their playfulness, so unleash your imagination, get silly, and have fun—they will, too.

Give praise. Reward children often with your praise—for how strong they are, how tough, how uncomplaining, how resourceful, and so forth. And occasionally, just for being there.

Be patient, patient, patient. You must be willing to linger at the wonderful frog pond beside the trail. Or to repeatedly tie a shoelace that won't stay tied. Or to answer whether mountains grow like trees. Or to listen to observations regarding an anthill. Or to explain for the eighteenth time when you're going to get there. And when your patience finally fails and you scream that unless everyone moves faster you won't make it home before next Christmas, then you must be patient and forgiving of yourself.

Food, Clothing, and Equipment

Food. The amount of food you take will depend on the length of the trip and the size of the party, but be sure your choices provide energy and nutrition; are compact, lightweight, and resistant to rough handling; and taste good. The latter is especially important when hiking with children, for while adults will readily eat any gruesome glop in the name of trail nutrition, children will rebel and often would rather starve first. Base your planning on family favorites that meet as many of the above criteria as possible; this is a good opportunity to involve children in trip planning. In New Mexico, avoid anything that melts readily, such as chocolate or cheese. Avoid salty foods, which increase water need; at the same time, encourage children to drink water often (see **Heat and water** in the Safety section, below). Some of the best trail foods I've found include raisins, dried apricots, carrot sticks, minimally sweetened cookies, salt-free gorp, virtually any fruit, graham crackers, and nuts.

Clothing. The trip and the season will determine the clothing you'll take, and parents don't need to be told how to dress their children for possible bad weather. Persons new to New Mexico, however, should remember the intensity of the sun and wear broad-brimmed hats and light and loose clothing for arms and legs during the warmer months. Though New Mexico's overall climate is arid, during the summer "monsoon season," July through August, thundershowers can occur

Goofing off at a campsite in Domingo Baca Canyon

nearly every day, usually in the afternoon, so each member of the party should have a poncho or rain slicker. Furthermore, while New Mexico is perceived as a warm state, local conditions vary enormously and the state's weather is notoriously fickle. The low humidity and consequent rapid evaporation mean that a person who gets soaked can become chilled easily, so it's wise to pack warm clothing as well as water-resistant clothing. (Leave your umbrellas at home, however; New Mexicans regard them as an east-of-the-Mississippi oddity.)

Ultimately, your goal should be for the children to be responsible for packing their own clothing, but you should realize this could be a very gradual process—and do lots of spot-checking in the meantime. I've opened a child's pack to find four stuffed animals—and no socks. And let's face it, checklists and cross-checking are good strategy even for adults-only hikes.

Boots. For many hikes in this book, running shoes or sneakers are adequate, but for longer hikes and backpack trips, boots are a must. They can be expensive, though newer styles substituting fabric for leather are less costly and also tend to be more comfortable and easier to break in. Good fit is essential; this is not the time to buy boots two sizes too big in anticipation of the child growing into them. As with your own boots, allow for two pairs of socks—a thin liner and a thicker outer sock. The boots must be broken in before a trip; have the child wear them around the house for several days until their comfort is assured. On a hike, battered but comfortable tennies are better than stiff and sturdy boots that don't fit.

Packs. Children's packs are readily available, with a wide range of prices and styles. When considering buying a pack, remember that children don't outgrow packs as rapidly as they do other equipment, so quality is more important. Conversely, there's less trauma in replacing an inexpensive pack that was lost, trodden in the dirt, or accidentally kicked into a camp fire. Whichever course you take, comfort and convenience—in that order—are paramount. Have the child try the pack on, preferably with a load.

On the trail, check with the child to make sure the pack is comfortable. A pack stuffed with pliable and light clothing will ride better than one half full of heavy, odd-shaped food items. The fat pack also will be a morale booster for a youngster who judges the status of a pack by its size, not its weight.

The Ten Essentials, Plus One

The Mountaineers, a long-established and respected hiking club in the Pacific Northwest, has compiled a list of ten items that every hike should include to allow you to cope better with unforeseen conditions or emergencies. To these "Ten Essentials" I've added an eleventh because of New Mexico's environment.

1. Extra clothing. New Mexico's weather can change rapidly, and children, who love to splash in mud puddles, wade through streams, and play in the sand, have their own techniques for needing extra clothing. Also, the possibility of unforeseen bad weather—or getting lost—makes it imperative for adults to pack appropriate extra clothing.

2. Extra food. Carry enough food so that if your hike lasts longer than expected, for whatever reason, you and your family won't go hungry.

3. Sun protection. Hat, sunglasses, sunscreen.

4. Pocketknife. The multifunction type is useful in countless situations. The tweezers on these knives find frequent use in pulling out tiny cactus prickers.

5. Firestarter candle or chemical fuel. Even in the desert, nights can be cold. Practice making a fire with these before you need them in an emergency.

6. Matches in a waterproof container. Look for waterproof matches in outing stores. Disposable lighters are a good backup.

7. First-aid kit and snakebite kit. Keep them complete, and learn how to use what's in them. In your first-aid kit, be sure to take any medications your children may need. And make sure before the hike that your children won't have bad reactions to unfamiliar chemical products, such as sunscreens with high ratings.

8. Flashlight. Imagine walking down a trail in the dark with little children—without a light. Be sure the batteries are strong and the bulbs functional; when possible, carry extra batteries and bulbs. While children delight in carrying flashlights, they aren't necessarily mindful of conserving batteries, so keep a backup with an adult.

9. Map. Be sure you have the correct and current map for the hike.

10. Compass. Know how to use it with your map to orient yourself.

11. Extra water. No hiker in New Mexico should ever be without an adequate and assured source of drinking water.

As you prepare for the hike, encourage children to carry not only their own food and equipment but also some group supplies and food, especially something the children will deem important, such as a compass or a flashlight; this gives them a sense of contributing to the trip. But avoid overloading children's packs, even when they clamor to carry more, particularly if they are beginning hikers. As all hikers know, the difference between a good trip and a miserable one often is just a few extra pounds in a pack, and no child wants the humiliation of having to ask someone else to take some of the load. And keep your own loads reasonable, especially if you have very young children; after all, you might have to carry them as well. I remember vividly my orthopedist shaking his head in disgust after the weekend when I carried my five-year-old daughter on my shoulders while bearing a heavy pack as well. Also, take time at the beginning to make sure the weight in the child's pack is properly distributed; children have a maddening way of not telling you about a trouble spot until after a blister has formed.

Preparing for an Overnighter

Preparing to spend the night in the wilderness, often far from other humans, involves considerably more planning than a simple dayhike. There's much more at stake if you omit an essential item. Below is a checklist I've developed for my family. They don't carry all the items on any given trip. Be selective—and keep your packs light:

Tents with rain flies
Sleeping bags
Foam pads
Portable stove
Fuel in fuel container
Flashlights and batteries
Waterproof matches and/or
  a disposable lighter

Cook set
Hot pads
Sponge and scrub pads
Detergent (try not to use it)
Can opener
Mugs
Food for three or more
  meals a day

Water in canteens or
    water bottles
Clothing
Socks (liners and outers,
    two of each)
Underwear
T-shirts or turtlenecks,
    preferably noncotton
Long pants and shorts
Swimsuits
Sweaters or sweatshirts
Jackets
Mittens or gloves
Hats
Bandannas, at least
    two each
Extra shoes
Raingear
Toilet paper
First-aid kit
Aspirin
Non-aspirin pain reliever
Adhesive bandages
Moleskin
First-aid cream
Antacid pills
Antidiarrheal medication
Water purification pills
Family medicines
Pocketknife and utility knife

Binoculars
Camera and film
Compass
Maps, including topo, highway,
    and U.S. Forest Service
Guidebooks for wildflowers,
    birds, stars, etc.
Notebook and pens
Sunscreen
Insect repellent
Extra glasses
Watch
Whistles
Zippable plastic bags
Sewing kit
Nylon cord
Walking stick
Backpack, fanny pack
Extra car key
Kids' supplies
Money and credit cards
Toiletries
Toothpaste and toothbrushes
Lotion
Sanitary napkins
Soap
Hairbrushes and combs
Towels and washcloths
Disposable premoistened towels

Outdoor Manners

Children learn good manners in the outdoors, as they learn them elsewhere, from adults.

Pack it out. The hiker's motto should be "Leave trails and campsites as clean as or cleaner than you found them." Sometimes it's good for children not only to help clean up their own campsites but also to clean up litter left by others; children form strong opinions about littering after picking up someone else's trash.

Explain about biodegradability and why things such as bottles, cans, aluminum foil, and even candy and gum wrappers can remain eyesores long after the litterers are gone. Zippable plastic bags in the parents' packs are convenient ways to handle hiking debris.

Personal hygiene. The "cat method" is recommended for disposing of human wastes. This consists of using a light digging tool, such as an aluminum garden trowel, to dig a hole 6 to 8 inches across and at least 6 inches deep; after defecating in the hole, refill the hole with loose soil and tramp it down. The hole should be at least 200 feet from campgrounds or water sources. Burying toilet paper with stools once was considered acceptable, but wild animals dig up the paper and strew it about, so pack it out in plastic bags. Don't burn it. Parents should check the children's toilet area to make sure they know how to do these things. Also, it's a good idea to pack a wet washcloth or disposable premoistened towels in a plastic bag for washing hands after toileting.

Dogs. Taking a dog on a hike, while usually a delight to children, should be discouraged. On the trail, the dog must be under control at all times so as not to threaten or hinder other hikers. At camp, the dog also must be under control so as not to bother other campers, whether by visiting their campsites or by chronic barking. And because dogs are predators, they can harass and kill wild birds and animals. What's more, domestic animals often behave unpredictably when suddenly placed in nature and may run away, which is certain to ruin any trip. My advice is to make everything much simpler by leaving the dog home, and besides, in many areas dogs are not allowed.

Stay on the trail. Avoid walking alongside the trail, to prevent trampling of vegetation. And don't allow children to shortcut switchbacks; water will follow their paths and erode the trail. Soil in the desert is especially fragile, because regeneration takes much longer than in more humid areas.

Tread softly. In arid regions, the soil often acquires a protective crust that, once disturbed, leaves the soil vulnerable to erosion. In areas of sandy soil, a complex living community of bacteria, fungi, and lichens forms. Called cryptobiotic crust or cryptogamic soil, this living soil has a distinctive dark, lumpy appearance. It takes 100 to 200 years for even a thin layer of this crust to develop. Avoid stepping or making camps on this inconspicuous but important part of desert ecology.

Camp fires. Most serious hikers today use portable stoves for cooking, but let's face it, a propane flame never will replace a wood fire for roasting marshmallows or telling camp stories. If you want a camp fire to be part of your camping experience, follow these guidelines: Keep any fire small, and build only in existing fire rings and only where it's safe and legally permitted. Some areas may prohibit all campfires during times of high forest-fire danger. Be sure to build your fire away from tents, trees, branches, brush, or other vegetation. Leave saws and axes at home; if there isn't abundant deadwood that you can gather outside the camp area, then don't make a fire. Burn all wood completely to ashes; fortunately, the climate's dryness usually makes that easy. Then, after dowsing the ashes with water or soil, test with your bare hands to make sure no coals remain. Finally, scatter or bury the ashes.

Don't feed wild animals. This not only disrupts wildlife ecology and encourages animals to become dependent on humans, it also exposes children to the possibility of bites and infection by animal-borne diseases, such as plague. (See **Plague and hantavirus**, under the section on Safety.)

Archaeological Sites

American Indians have lived in New Mexico for more than 13,000 years; indeed, the Clovis group, the oldest widely accepted prehistoric culture in the New World, takes its name from a site in New Mexico. Paleo-Indian sites such as Clovis are rare and inconspicuous, but

Indian feet wore grooves into the volcanic tuff at Tsankawi Ruins.

sometime around A.D. 1000 a culture suddenly blossomed that led to the most impressive pre-Columbian structures north of Mexico. We don't know what these people called themselves, so we refer to them as Ancestral Puebloans, because their descendants are found among today's Pueblo Indians. Though it's still unclear why the Ancestral Puebloans abandoned their settlements in the Four Corners area or exactly what became of them, it's all but certain at least some of their descendants are among the inhabitants of modern pueblos at Hopi, Zuni, Laguna, Acoma, and along the Rio Grande.

Many hikes in this book are centered on Ancestral Puebloan archaeological sites, which impose special hazards and responsibilities. For example, the Ancestral Puebloan ruins are at least 600 years old, and most are much older; they are a priceless and irreplaceable part of our heritage. These ruins, by their very nature, are precarious and fragile; to protect children and also to protect the ruins, children must not climb or scramble on them. And while children love to search for pottery sherds and flint chips, all archaeological artifacts should be left in place, as artifacts lose their scientific value when removed from their original location. Similarly, parents should take care to keep children from scratching their names on or otherwise defacing petroglyphs, the pictures pecked into stone by the ancient Indians. Instead, find an appropriate loose stone back at the campsite and let the children try creating their own petroglyphs there. Take time before the hike to discuss with children why archaeological artifacts and sites deserve— and need—our respect and protection, and reiterate this at the sites themselves.

Safety

Any party hiking with children in New Mexico should be aware of several potential hazards not necessarily found in other regions. Those listed below should be taken into account on most hikes, in most seasons, and thus are not listed for the specific hikes.

Getting lost. The strategies for keeping children from getting lost are simple: Have the party stay together, stay on the trail, always wait for everyone at trail junctions, and be familiar with directions and landmarks. But despite these precautions, anyone, adults included, can occasionally get turned around and discover that things aren't where they thought they were. Children especially need to be taught what to do when this happens. Each person in a party should have a loud whistle. If a person becomes lost, he or she should not panic but should stay put and summon help by using the whistle to blow the international distress signal—three loud blasts. Children should repeat this until help arrives. Kids will want to practice a few times with their whistles, but emphasize that the whistles are not toys but are to be used only in genuine emergencies. Another rule is always to let someone know where you're going. This applies to the entire party leaving word at a ranger station before going on a hike and also to children letting you know before going off to gather pine cones.

Heat and water. Heat avoidance and water management are critical for successful hiking in New Mexico. Midday temperatures often exceed 100 degrees Fahrenheit in the summer in many parts of the state, yet you can hike year-round in comfort simply by skill-fully choosing when and where to hike. In the summer, my family heads north and into the high mountains. When we can't do that, we hike in the early morning or late evening; the climate's low humidity means little moisture to hold the heat of midday.

But this low humidity also evaporates sweat rapidly, making it seem you're perspiring less than you actually are. In such climates, the water loss from a person exercising outdoors during the summer can be enormous. And research has shown that even mild dehydration can affect physical stamina. Thus, take ample water and drink early and often; encourage children to drink *before* they're thirsty. Two quarts to a gallon per day per person is appropriate for long, strenuous hikes or desert hikes; a quart per person usually is enough for hikes not exceeding 4 hours. And don't hoard water supplies until the end of the hike; as the saying goes, the best place to store water is in your stomach.

When convenient, have children carry their own water bottles and canteens; this makes water readily available and also builds responsibility and self-sufficiency. As for water in springs or streams, *Giardia* has been found throughout the state, though it's nowhere common. Filtration or boiling for 20 minutes are the only precautions against this parasite.

Aside from general discomfort and fatigue, the main heat hazard is heatstroke, a very serious condition that can occur quite suddenly. Its symptoms include hot, flushed, dry skin; dilated pupils; rapid pulse; and often mental sluggishness and disorientation. Take the victim to a cool and shady place, encourage calm and inaction, and reduce body temperature by removing clothing and dousing with water.

The sun. Three factors make hikers in New Mexico especially vulnerable to skin damage from the sun's ultraviolet rays: southern latitude, putting the sun high in the sky; little atmospheric moisture to block harmful rays; and an average elevation of about 1 mile above sea level, meaning much less atmospheric protection than at lower elevations. Elevation is the most influential factor, meaning that protection is most important on high-country trips. Protection also is most needed during the 4-hour period when the sun is most directly overhead.

My children still grumble occasionally when I tell them at the beginning of a hike to smear gooey sunscreen on their exposed skin, but they've nonetheless come to accept that for fair-skinned families such as ours, sunscreen rated 15 or above is the best alternative to a painful sunburn.

Flash floods. Until you've seen a flash flood, its suddenness and ferocity are difficult to imagine, especially on sunny days when only sand fills the arroyos. Don't let children play in arroyos, dry washes, or shallow streams on stormy days, and on such days be mindful of escape routes.

Rattlesnakes. Rattlesnakes are found throughout New Mexico at elevations below 8,000 feet (give or take a thousand feet). And while the odds are against seeing a rattlesnake on any given trip, that doesn't make the odd encounter any less disturbing, especially when children are present.

If you are truly terrified of rattlesnakes—don't apologize if you are—then avoid them entirely by taking your high-country trips during months with warm nighttime temperatures and exploring the lower elevations in cooler months. You'll also avoid the heat.

Otherwise, warn children that they're in rattlesnake country and tell them not to put their hands or feet where they can't see. Never touch a "dead" snake; rattlesnakes will lie completely motionless for long periods, and even dead snakes have residual reflexes that can result in a bite. Also, never tease or poke a snake with a stick. My children and I have encountered numerous rattlesnakes on our hikes— we've even inadvertently stepped over them. I'm convinced the snakes do not want to bite if they can avoid it. But I also must report that rattlesnakes cannot be relied upon to rattle as a warning of their presence.

If a bite does occur, take the following steps: 1) Don't panic; children will model their behavior after yours. 2) Wash the affected area. 3) As efficiently as possible, apply constriction above the bite, being careful not to hinder the circulation of blood. The purpose of the tourniquet is to prevent the spread of venom just beneath the skin; you should feel pulses beyond the site of the bite. 4) With a flame-sterilized blade make small, linear (parallel to veins) incisions ⅛- to ¼-inch deep and ½- to ¾-inch long at the bite marks and suck out as much venom as possible. Note: Venom is not injected with each bite. If you're uncertain, wait 3 to 5 minutes and watch for pain and swelling before taking measures. 5) As quickly as possible, get the victim to a hospital, where antivenin is available. Keep the victim as calm and inactive as possible; carry a small child. And repeatedly remind yourself and the victim that, with prompt action, the odds are overwhelmingly in your favor. Snakebite kits with detailed instructions are available in most outdoor stores. More detailed instructions on field treatment of snakebites can be found in *Medicine for Mountaineering* (The Mountaineers, 1992).

Spiders. Two species of poisonous spiders are found in New Mexico: the brown recluse and the black widow. Both are retiring and nonaggressive, and most bites occur when a spider has gotten into clothing or bedding. Symptoms of a bite include pain centered on a red area. But if you suspect a bite has occurred, do not wait for symptoms. Seek medical help immediately. Countermeasures are available.

Both species are most often found around human dwellings and not in wild nature. I've never seen either on a hiking trip in New Mexico. I have, however, seen several tarantulas, and fortunate indeed is the trip in which children get to observe one of these hairy giants stalking along the ground. But don't attempt to touch tarantulas or trap them. Their bite, while not lethal, is painful and subject to infection—and tarantulas are not intimidated by humans.

Scorpions. Scorpions are found throughout the warmer regions of New Mexico, yet their retiring habits make the chances of being stung by one remote. What's more, the lethal species isn't found in the state. When camping, don't leave clothing, shoes, or bedding out, and shake these out before using them. Most scorpion stings occur

The cones of the piñon pine yield edible nuts.

when humans lift stones or logs and touch the scorpion underneath. The sting of a nonlethal scorpion is similar to, though somewhat more severe than, that of a bee or wasp and should be treated similarly. If stung, apply ice to the affected area if possible. In all our hikes throughout New Mexico, my family has encountered only one scorpion, a dormant one we uncovered in a dirt bank.

Stickers and prickers. Children seem to have a natural affinity for cacti, and locating unusual species along the trail is one of the delights of hiking with children in New Mexico. But stumbling into a cholla or a prickly pear cactus can be extremely painful and terrifying. The spines can be removed, with difficulty, by using tweezers and fingers. In the fall, children love to sample the reddish edible fruits of the prickly pear cactus, but the fruit has on its skin tiny hairlike stickers. So handle the fruit carefully, and peel it before eating it; the stickers may be small, but they can be a stubborn annoyance if stuck in fingers or tongue. I remove the stickers with the tweezers in my pocketknife.

Poison ivy. This plant occurs in scattered, usually moist locations, and children should be taught to identify it as soon as possible. I've done this with a game, promising a reward to whomever can spot a poison ivy plant. My kids love this, and their plant identification skills have increased rapidly. If you happen to touch poison ivy, you can remove much of the toxic oil, or at least mitigate its spread, by scrubbing with strong soap within 5 to 10 minutes after contact. The rash triggered by poison ivy appears four to seven days after contact and disappears in about the same length of time. Resist scratching the itch. Treatment varies according to the severity of the reaction; consult a physician. Though my family and I routinely encounter poison ivy on our hikes, we've only once experienced a reaction—and that was when one of us put the beautiful red fall foliage in a bouquet!

Stinging nettle. This plant occurs occasionally along streams, and children and adults should learn to recognize it. Contact with stinging nettle results in mild to moderate skin pain that disappears in an hour or less.

Theft. Sad to say, theft and vandalism are increasingly common at trailheads in New Mexico. Always lock your vehicle, and don't tempt thieves by leaving camping gear or valuables exposed. If you must leave a parked car for several days, make sure valuable articles are concealed, and ask local officials to check on it during patrols in the area.

Plague and hantavirus. Bumperstickers in New Mexico facetiously proclaim the state to be "home of the flea, land of the plague." The *Yersinia pestis* bacillus, which causes plague, is endemic to New Mexico. Modern medicine is not helpless against plague, but this still is a devastating disease and should be taken seriously. Fortunately, cases are rare, and the precautions simple and effective: Avoid all contact with wild animals, especially rodents such as prairie dogs, squirrels, chipmunks, and so forth. Avoid their holes and dens. Don't examine their dead bodies. Similarly, discourage contact between wild animals and your pets. Use flea collars, and dust with flea powder.

Important: If you live outside New Mexico and develop plague symptoms—high fever, swelling in armpits and groin—after returning home, tell your doctor that you've been in New Mexico and perhaps were exposed to plague. Outside the areas where plague occurs, few physicians would ever suspect plague, whose symptoms resemble those of other diseases, and early diagnosis is important.

The above cautions also apply to hantavirus, a serious disease that emerged in New Mexico in 1993 but since has been discovered elsewhere. The best protection is simply to avoid all contact with all rodents and their habitations.

A final caution. Scorpions, rattlesnakes, poison ivy, flash floods, plague—together they're enough to make you wonder whether you're better off taking your children to a city park and forgetting about the outdoors until they're old enough to defend themselves. I wish I could tell you the above hazards are so rare that you can forget about them, but regrettably the dangers are real: In more than ten years of hiking together in New Mexico, my family has encountered rattlesnakes, scorpions, poison ivy, and flash floods. None of us has ever been bitten or stung, but rattlesnake warnings took on new meaning for me after I watched my daughters run down a trail and unknowingly leap over one.

Still, on any given trip the odds are overwhelming that nothing scary will happen, and the only sure way to avoid exposing your children to natural hazards is not to venture into nature—and thus miss all the joy and revelation that await you there.

That's the greatest danger of all.

A Note About Safety

Safety is an important concern in all outdoor activities. No guidebook can alert you to every hazard or anticipate the limitations of every reader. Therefore, the descriptions of roads, trails, routes, and natural features in this book are not representations that a particular place or excursion will be safe for your party. When you follow any of the routes described in this book, you assume responsibility for your own safety. Under normal conditions, such excursions require the usual attention to traffic, road and trail conditions, weather, terrain, the capabilities of your party, and other factors. Keeping informed on current conditions and exercising common sense are the keys to a safe, enjoyable outing.

New Mexico for Nonresidents (and even Some Residents)

New Mexico is mostly desert, right? After all, the photos most nonresidents see are of the dunes at White Sands, or the parched ruins in Chaco Canyon, or the dusty homes made of sun-baked adobe. What's more, Interstate 40, the major east-west route through the state, reinforces this impression as it enters on the arid eastern plains and exits into Arizona at the scenic but dry mesas near Gallup.

New Mexico does have a dry climate; 90 percent of the state receives less than 20 inches of precipitation annually, while 20 percent to 30 percent of the state receives less than 10 inches.

And New Mexico does have deserts; in fact, large portions of the state are part of the Sonoran or Chihuahuan Desert life zones. But the state also has lakes, waterfalls, mountain ranges, alpine meadows, fertile grasslands, and vast areas of forest. Indeed, New Mexico has more forest than most states in the Midwest.

This incredible and often unpredictable diversity is the state's greatest natural characteristic and, for hikers, a source of endless delight. The hikes in this book include recent lava flows (the Zuni-Acoma Trail, hike 44), high-country lakes (Williams Lake, hike 4, and Middle Fork Lake, hike 3), enormous sand dunes (White Sands, hike 50), mesas (Tsankawi Ruins, hike 17), badlands (the Bisti, hike 41), mountain crests (Tree Spring Trail, hike 30), high meadows (White Mountain Wilderness Crest, hike 49), and much, much more. If children balk at walking another path in the woods, propose going underground and exploring a lava tube (El Calderon Crater, hike 45).

The diversity of landscapes and climate zones also means you can hike somewhere in the state at virtually any time of the year. When summer's heat makes southern New Mexico an oven during the day, you can head for the cool high country of the Jemez Mountains or the Sangre de Cristo Mountains. When it's March and you're sick of winter in northern New Mexico, you can head south, to the Organ Mountains or White Sands, and hike in shirt sleeves.

To understand a little of this diverse landscape it's perhaps best to start with the natural forces that have shaped that landscape. As elsewhere, erosion is the foremost of these. New Mexico has several rivers: the Pecos, heading in the Sangre de Cristo Mountains east of Santa Fe and running southeast; the Chama, heading in Colorado and flowing south to join the Rio Grande; the Canadian, heading in the northeastern part of the state and flowing southeast into Texas; the San Juan, heading in Colorado and flowing west and north back into Colorado; and the Gila and the San Francisco, heading in the southwestern part of the state and flowing southwest into Arizona.

But New Mexico's greatest river—its Spanish name means "great river"—is the Rio Grande, traversing the entire central length of the state. In the north, it has carved deep, narrow canyons with vertiginous walls, such as the spectacular Rio Grande Gorge near Taos. Farther south, beginning about Albuquerque, the Rio Grande flows through a broad valley extending all the way to Mexico; in this valley is much of the state's agriculture.

Along the southern Rio Grande and throughout southwestern New Mexico is the true basin and range country of the American West. Here the valleys are caused not only by erosion but also by subsidence of huge fault blocks, accompanied by uplift of other fault blocks, creating a pattern of linear, north-south trending mountain ranges separated by broad, open basins. As you drive south on Interstate 25, paralleling the Rio Grande, you'll see several of these mountain ranges along the valley—the Fra Cristobal Range, the Caballo Range, the San Andres Mountains, and the Organ Mountains.

Water has been important in shaping the landscape in other ways as well, not only eroding the rocks but also creating them. Throughout the state are sedimentary strata laid down when oceans covered much

Hiker next to one of the caves for which Cave Creek was named

of what is now New Mexico. The weathering of these strata has created the impressive mesas, buttes, and pillars that are such a characteristic part of the Southwest. The remains of these ancient seas are particularly well displayed in the northwestern part of the state, with its spectacular mesas and badlands, many of which are famous for the fossils they contain.

But as you drive along just about any highway in New Mexico you're sure to see evidence of the other force responsible for the present landscape—volcanism. Except for the southeastern plains, reminders of the state's volcanic history are everywhere: cinder cones such as Capulin Mountain National Monument in the northeast; black buttes such as Cerro Tome along the Rio Grande; mesas capped with black lava like those at Petroglyph National Monument near Albuquerque; eroded volcanic plugs like Shiprock in the northwest; compressed layers of volcanic ash such as Tent Rocks in the Jemez Mountains; hot springs like McCauley Hot Spring; and many more. The mountains of the sprawling Gila Wilderness in the southwestern part of the state are the remnants of long-vanished volcanoes, as are the Jemez Mountains in the north-central part of the state. *Malpais*, "bad country," is the Spanish word that in New Mexico refers to lava flows, and Valley of Fires State Park near Carrizozo and El Malpais National Monument feature spectacular lava flows, some only 1,000 years old. While no volcanoes currently are active in New Mexico, geologists assure us this is but a temporary lull. In fact, they even predict where the next volcanism will occur: near Socorro, where a magma chamber has been detected expanding beneath the earth's surface.

While water and volcanism have been the most powerful forces shaping the landscape, wind has been important, too. The dunes of White Sands and the strange landforms of northwestern New Mexico, such as Angel Peak southeast of Farmington, owe their existence to the action of strong winds.

While it's possible to make some generalizations about New Mexico's climate, for hiking purposes it's better to think of microclimates, as the diversity of local conditions can be dramatic. In Albuquerque, for example, it's not uncommon in the winter to ski in the mountains in the morning and play tennis in town in the afternoon. And in March, spring wildflowers are blooming in the Guadalupe Mountains while the Sangre de Cristo Mountains are still accumulating their annual snowpack. Because of the intensity of sunlight here, day to night fluctuations in temperature are greater than in most other regions of the country. Temperatures can dip well below freezing at night yet soar into the 60s when the sun is out. Cross-country skiers here know very well that south-facing slopes can be bare of snow, while north-facing slopes have snow requiring cold wax.

For hikers and campers, a few guidelines might be helpful:

Expect deep snow to restrict access to the higher elevations of the Sangre de Cristo Mountains until late May or even mid-June.

Throughout most of New Mexico, May and June are relatively dry; so are late September, October, and November.

The wettest months are July and August—New Mexico's so-called "monsoon season"—when an influx of moisture-laden tropical air results in frequent and sometimes violent afternoon thundershowers. In the high mountains, these can occur nearly every day, so hikers hoping to climb peaks or ridges during monsoon season should plan to be off the peaks by noon. Also, persons hiking and camping during these months should be prepared for heavy rain.

New Mexico also has a windy season, typically in late March and early April, when strong westerlies fill the air with dust and grit. Not pleasant for hiking, especially in exposed areas.

Barring storms, winter can yield some surprisingly good hiking, especially in the southern part of the state. Snow rarely lingers, and daytime temperatures in the bright sun are quite pleasant.

Because of the low humidity, the air warms up and cools off quite quickly; torrid afternoons fade rapidly into pleasant evenings, while chilly nights soon melt into warm days.

A New Mexico Vocabulary

For most of its history since European peoples arrived, New Mexico was governed by a Spanish-speaking nation, first Spain and then Mexico; today Spanish is recognized along with English as an official language in the state. Because Spanish speakers were the first European explorers and colonizers in New Mexico, it's hardly surprising that maps of New Mexico are filled with Spanish terms for natural features. Below is a brief glossary of Spanish terms that hikers are likely to encounter; many terms commonly have a diminutive form, such as *-ito*, *-ita*, *-illo*, or *-illa*:

Agua, water, sometimes used synonymously with streams and springs

Arroyo, a watercourse or erosional channel, usually small, usually dry

Bosque, bosquecito, forest, usually referring more specifically to the dense vegetation along a stream or river

Caliente, hot, often descriptive of springs

Cañada, canyon, deep valley, gully

Cañon, cañoncito, canyon, deep valley

Ceja, brow, ridge, crest of a hill

Cerro, cerrito, cerrillo, hill, though in New Mexico some sizable mountains have this term applied to them

Cienega, cieneguilla, swamp, marsh

Cuchilla, literally "knife," but also referring metaphorically to a ridge

Cuesta, cuestecito, ridge

Cumbre, summit

Fria, cold, applied descriptively to water bodies

Ladera, slope, side of a mountain

Laguna, lagunita, lake

Llano, llanito, plain

Loma, lomita, hill

Malpais, literally "bad country," but usually referring specifically to lava flows

Mesa, mesita, mesilla, literally "table," but also referring to any flat-topped landform, whether a distinct feature or a more general region, such as the flat land above a river

Ojo, ojito, spring

Picacho, peak

Playa, beach, but also referring to a dry, sandy area

Potrero, a finger-shaped mesa extending from a larger feature

Puerto, puerta, puertecito, gap, pass

Rincon, rinconada, box canyon

Rio, river, though some very small streams carry this appellation in New Mexico!

Rito, creek

Sierra, range of mountains

Vado, ford

Valle, vallecito, valley, basin

Key to Symbols

 Dayhikes. These are hikes that can be completed in a single day. While some trips allow camping, only a few require it.

 Backpack trips. These are hikes whose length or difficulty makes camping out either necessary or recommended for most families.

 Easy trails. These are relatively short, smooth, gentle trails suitable for small children or first-time hikers.

 Moderate trails. Most of these are 2 to 4 miles total distance and feature more than 500 feet of elevation gain. The trail may be rough and uneven. Hikers should wear lug-soled boots and be sure to carry the Ten Essentials.

 Difficult trails. These are often rough, with considerable elevation gain or distance to travel. They are suitable for older or experienced children. Lug-soled boots and the Ten Essentials are standard equipment.

 Hikable. The best times of year to hike each trail are indicated by the following symbols: flower—spring; sun—summer; leaf—fall; snowflake—winter.

Northern New Mexico

A high-country lake in the Sangre de Cristo Mountains

1. Columbine Canyon

Type: Dayhike
Difficulty: Easy for children
Hikable: May through October
One way: 2 miles
Starting elevation: 7,780 feet
High point: 8,700 feet
Maps: Latir Peak and Wheeler Peak Wildernesses (Carson National Forest); Questa 7.5-minute USGS quad
Hazards: None

As you hike this trail in the Sangre de Cristo Mountains, make a game of having your children count the different wildflower species you encounter, and give a prize to anyone spotting the columbines that gave this canyon its name. The columbines you're likely to see in bloom June through August are the red-yellow variety, not the blue ones more common farther north, but perhaps you'll be lucky. And

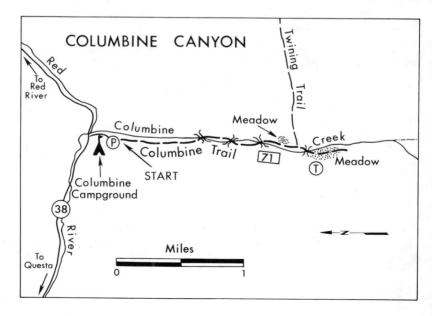

even when the columbines are not in bloom, numerous other mountain wildflowers—Arizona rose, thimbleberry, Oregon grape, yarrow, geranium, elderberry—make this easy hike along Columbine Creek in the Carson National Forest worthwhile.

To reach the creek, drive on NM 38 for 5.4 miles east from its junction with NM 522 in Questa to the Carson National Forest Columbine Campground. (Several other national forest campgrounds are located along the Red River.) As you drive you'll follow the Red River, named for its ruddy color during spring runoff. Late in the last century, the mountains were the focus of intense prospecting and mining. Just opposite the Columbine Campground, on the north side of the road, are huge earthworks created by mining for molybdenum.

The Columbine Canyon Trail, U.S. Forest Service Trail 71, begins at the back, or south end, of the Columbine Campground; there are parking spaces here. The trailhead is marked with a sign labeling the Columbine-Twining National Recreation Trail, which coincides with Trail 71. During the mining boom, Columbine Canyon was a route used by miners and prospectors traveling between the gold camps of the Red River Valley and the mining camp of Twining, now the Taos Ski Valley, to the south. The Columbine Canyon Trail follows the old route. As you hike ask children to imagine early prospectors traveling over this trail with shovels, picks, and gold pans loaded onto horses or mules, or, if the miners weren't so fortunate, carried in crude canvas packs very unlike the lightweight gear we use today. Along the way they would have paused to scoop gravel from Columbine Creek and wash it in their gold pans, searching for tiny flecks of yellow. They found few, if any.

From the trailhead at Columbine Campground, the Columbine

A small natural dam on Columbine Creek

Canyon Trail climbs gradually through spruce-fir-aspen forest for about 0.5 mile before descending to join Columbine Creek, which it crosses over a footbridge. If you see columbines as you hike, have children examine the spurs of the flower's petals, said to resemble an eagle's claws. From these came the flower's scientific genus name *Aquilegia*, from the Latin word for eagle. The common name, columbine, comes from another Latin word, *columba*, meaning "dove." Ask children if the petals remind them of a group of doves clustered together.

From the footbridge, the trail remains close to the stream, passing beneath jagged cliffs to the east. After two more footbridges, about 0.25 mile apart, the trail arrives at a small meadow. Just beyond this, where a log footbridge spans a tiny stream, Trail 72, called the Twining Trail, branches left and uphill. This trail is steep and difficult; after about 11 miles it arrives at Twining. Just beyond the Columbine-Twining trail junction, the Columbine Trail crosses Columbine Creek yet again and enters another small meadow and aspen grove. This is a natural turnaround point, a delightful place for a picnic. The trail continues along Columbine Creek, though it soon begins to get steeper, and after about 4 miles it crosses an 11,200-foot divide, where it becomes Trail 60 and descends into Hondo Canyon just west of Twining.

But if you go no farther than the little meadow, you'll have had a pleasant excursion in the Sangre de Cristo Mountains, and the wildflowers you'll have seen will have been far more colorful and abundant than the gold the miners sought.

2. Red River Nature Trail

Type:	Dayhike
Difficulty:	Easy to moderate for children
Hikable:	May through October
One way:	2 miles
Starting elevation:	8,640 feet
High point:	9,020 feet
Map:	Red River 7.5-minute USGS quad
Hazards:	None

This is one of New Mexico's best nature trails—readily accessible, easy yet long enough for a satisfying hike, scenic, with intelligent and interesting interpretive markers.

The trail parallels the southwest bank of the Red River as it flows past the village of Red River. It can be reached at several points in the village, but the easiest access is simply to turn southwest on Pioneer Road from the village's main street. Pioneer Road leads to the ski lifts, and the nature trail starts on the southwest side of the road immediately after the road crosses the bridge over the Red River, just a couple of blocks from the main street. Because there's limited parking near the trailhead, you might want to park downtown and simply walk along Pioneer Road to the trailhead. When you've crossed the bridge, walk between the red ski lift and the river to a marker indicating the nature trail's start. From here the trail follows the river's southwest bank.

As you hike, children will enjoy looking for upcoming interpretive markers. Across the river is the village, and above are the mine-scarred hills recalling the village's early history as a mining boomtown. The trail passes by what remains of the Copper King mine, one of the region's first.

After about 0.75 mile the trail begins to ascend. This is a good place for a break, or if you've had enough hiking at this point, simply leave the trail, head northeast, cross the river over a footbridge, and join the village at the Y-junction with NM 38 and NM 578.

If you continue hiking, you begin climbing the mountain's slopes,

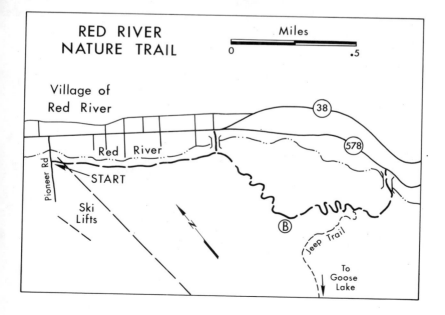

A bridge over the Red River

and after several switchbacks you reach the trail's highest point, where a bench awaits hikers. From here the trail descends steeply on more switchbacks. The trail sometimes is obscure and confusing here, especially as it passes near the jeep road leading uphill to Goose Lake. The trail ends at the road just after a log bridge over a tiny stream, but if at any point you become confused simply follow the road downhill; it will lead you to a footbridge over the Red River. Just beyond is NM 578. From here a 0.7-mile walk along the highway takes you back to the Y and the village of Red River. Be careful of traffic as you walk with children along the highway. Or during the summer, you can wait for a trolley, which stops at the highway where you've come out, and ride that back to the village.

Note: Another hike children will love in Red River is taking the red ski lift to the mountain's top and then hiking along the open crest. The lift ascends 1,515 feet in 1.1 miles. When you're done hiking and enjoying the spectacular views you can ride back down.

3. Middle Fork Lake

Type:	Dayhike or backpack
Difficulty:	Moderate for children
Hikable:	June through September
One way:	2.25 miles
Starting elevation:	9,650 feet
High point:	10,875 feet
Maps:	Latir Peak and Wheeler Peak Wildernesses (Carson National Forest); Wheeler Peak 7.5-minute USGS quad
Hazards:	None

The trout are large and numerous in Middle Fork Lake, and its setting in the shadows of the high peaks of the Sangre de Cristo Mountains is spectacular. It's good both as a dayhike and as an easily accessible overnighter, and its elevation at nearly 11,000 feet gives children a good opportunity to experience the beautiful and interesting subalpine ecosystem.

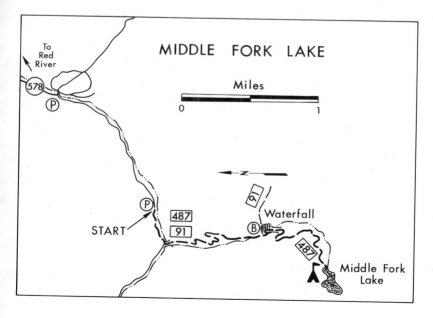

A waterfall and a stream crossing on the way to Middle Fork Lake

The trailhead is reached by driving south on paved NM 578 from the village of Red River from its intersection with NM 38 at the south end of town. Drive 6.4 miles to the pavement's end (don't cross the bridge on right). Park here or drive another 1.1 miles over the narrow, rocky, and sometimes wet unpaved road to the right—a sign indicates this to be the route to Middle Fork Lake—to a Carson National Forest parking area. Jeeps and high-clearance four-wheel-drive vehicles can drive all the way to the lake, but the road is steep and rough, with many tight switchbacks. Heavy use of the road by vehicles, especially on weekends, can be an annoyance to hikers; plan your trip for weekdays if possible.

From the parking area, hikers will follow the road about 0.25 mile, then cross the stream on a log bridge. Here the road coincides with Trails 487 and 91 and begins an uphill climb that will not cease until the lake is reached 2 miles later.

As you hike you'll glimpse small waterfalls along the stream, but after 1 mile you'll come to a much more scenic waterfall, a natural place for a break. Here the road crosses the stream, but hikers will take the log bridge, then continue on the road as it switchbacks steadily uphill 1 long mile to the lake. Though the total distance is not great, small hikers, particularly those unaccustomed to high altitudes, will consider this section taxing. The best strategy is to move slowly and take frequent breaks. Tell children that even the strongest hikers can be affected by unaccustomed high altitude; after all, their bodies are used to more oxygen than they're getting from the air.

Also at the stream crossing and the waterfall, Trail 91 leaves Trail 487 to ascend the slopes to the east before turning south again, eventually heading into the Wheeler Peak Wilderness to Lost Lake. Followed still farther, this trail goes to Horseshoe Lake and from there to the summit of Wheeler Peak, at 13,161 feet the highest point in New Mexico. Trail 91 is a much longer, more difficult, and wilder trail than the route to Middle Fork Lake, but strong parties might want to consider this an alternative to Middle Fork Lake.

At Middle Fork Lake are numerous campsites for overnight stays. Unfortunately, easy access from Red River for jeeps and ATVs makes this lake a popular destination, especially during the summer, but Middle Fork Lake's beauty still makes the hike worthwhile.

Middle Fork Lake's elevation at almost 11,000 feet puts it in the subalpine life zone, with its wonderful array of high-country wildflowers, such as gentian, kings crown, marsh marigold, and snowball saxifrage. Ask children what unique challenges plants face in this environment. How do plants cope with the short growing season and the cool temperatures?

If you're lucky, you'll see some of the animals that live in this subalpine environment, such as marmots and coneys, also known as pikas. They, like the plants, have had to adopt special techniques for living here, where the winters are so long, such as storing energy as fat, growing thick insulating fur, and creating underground caches of food. Children may see where these animals have made piles of leaves and branches.

Return the way you came. Though it's tempting to shortcut the switchbacks, both your knees and the erodable soil will appreciate your staying on the prescribed route.

---

4. Williams Lake

Type: Dayhike
Difficulty: Moderate for children
Hikable: June through September
One way: 2.5 miles
Starting elevation: 9,960 feet
High point: 11,040 feet
Maps: Latir Peak and Wheeler Peak Wildernesses (Carson National Forest); Wheeler Peak 7.5-minute USGS quad
Hazards: None

At 13,161 feet, Wheeler Peak is New Mexico's highest mountain, and while this hike doesn't get you on top, it does put you at the

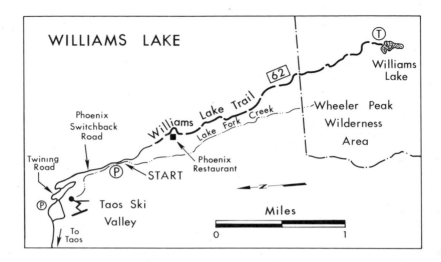

mountain's base and into the high country of the Wheeler Peak Wilderness—all for a modest amount of relatively easy hiking. What's more,
the trailhead is a short and very scenic drive from downtown Taos.

To reach the trailhead from Taos, drive north on US 64 for 3 miles
to NM 150, where signs indicate the Taos Ski Valley is 15 miles away.
Drive to the ski area, and as you enter it, look to your left, opposite
the resort complex, for a parking lot where a Carson National Forest
sign indicates the Wheeler Peak Wilderness access. Just a few yards
away is the dirt Twining Road. Drive on this, following signs to "Hiker
Parking," turning left onto Zaps Road, then right onto Kachina Road.
At the hiker parking area are information and picnic tables. Here,
you'll find signs indicating the route to Williams Lake. Continue following a rough dirt road on the east side of Lake Fork Creek. At about
0.25 mile from the restaurant, the main road crosses the creek, but
you should keep left. Soon you'll encounter a Carson National Forest
sign indicating Williams Lake Trail 62, Williams Lake 2 miles.

The trail ascends gradually but persistently as it goes up the
valley through spruce-fir forest. Children can learn to recognize spruce
by their needles being square in cross-section, while fir needles are
flat. Explain that the spruce-fir forest is a climax forest—a stable and
self-perpetuating forest community. Indeed, the spruce-fir zone is the
highest, wettest, windiest, and coldest of New Mexico's life zones in
which full-sized trees can live; above this, the trees are stunted, as
children will see around Williams Lake. To emphasize the harshness
of the climate here, have children notice the steep mountainsides to

your left and the tracks of winter avalanches. Shortly before reaching
the lake, the trail passes by huge mounds of boulders shoved there
by glacial ice.

Williams Lake lies in a basin surrounded by the jagged high peaks
of the Wheeler Peak Wilderness. Don't bring your fishing gear, as the
lake is very shallow. Camping and camp fires are not permitted around
the lakeshore. The trail continues east past Williams Lake, eventually
to the Wheeler Peak ridge, but beyond the lake the trail becomes very
steep.

Hikers with children likely will stop here to relax on the meadow
and admire the views of the surrounding peaks while children explore
the small lake. The mud flats around the lake sometimes have tracks
of wild animals, perhaps even bears and mountain lions. My wife and
I once found a bear track in mud near here. And at 11,000 feet the
lake is in New Mexico's subalpine zone, the transition between forest
and treeless tundra. The wildflowers in this zone are particularly
beautiful and interesting. Among my children's favorites are the small
pink flowers known as little red elephants, named because each flower
on the dense spike is shaped like an elephant's head, complete with
ears and uplifted trunk. Mention to children that because of the short
growing season at this high elevation, the plants must complete their
cycles quickly.

No one knows for sure how Williams Lake got its name, but this
little lake in the wilderness possibly recalls William S. Williams, an

Williams Lake and the high ridges of the Wheeler Peak Wilderness

ex-preacher who arrived in Taos in the fall of 1825 and joined the many other mountain men and trappers in the area. Wheeler Peak bears the name of Major George M. Wheeler, who was in charge of surveying the land west of the 100th meridian between 1871 and 1878. Wheeler Peak wasn't recognized as the state's tallest mountain until 1948. That's when a Santa Fe photographer, Harold D. Walter, made measurements that showed Wheeler is slightly higher than the Truchas Peaks to the south. All this land is part of the 19,663-acre Wheeler Peak Wilderness, administered by the Carson National Forest.

5. Palo Flechado Pass

Type:	Dayhike
Difficulty:	Easy for children
Hikable:	May through October
One way:	1.25 miles
Starting elevation:	8,540 feet
High point:	9,107 feet
Map:	Palo Flechado 7.5-minute USGS quad
Hazards:	None

The Spanish phrase *palo flechado* means "tree stuck with arrows," a name said to come either from a battle here that left a tree bristling with arrows or from a Taos Indian custom of shooting arrows into a tree following hunts on the eastern plains. But it's the scenic little pond that children and their parents likely will find most appealing about this short hike in the Carson National Forest.

The easiest, shortest way to do this hike is simply to drive on US 64 east of Taos to Palo Flechado Pass, which is marked by a historical information sign, drop hikers off at the pass, and then pick them up at the bottom. The trailhead isn't marked but is easy to find on the northeast side of the highway at the pass; the trail is an old, overgrown dirt road leading down through the forest. It's all downhill until the trail rejoins US 64, 1.25 miles away.

But for a slightly longer round-trip hike, park at the bottom. The trailhead and parking area, just inside the national forest boundary, are readily seen on the southwest side of US 64 about 1.5 miles west of its junction with NM 434, north of Angel Fire. No signs at the

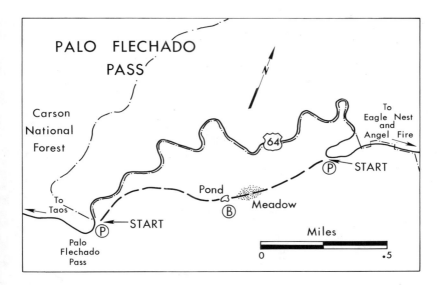

trailhead mention Palo Flechado Pass—they mention Bull Spring and Elliott Barker Camp—but don't worry; simply take the single, obvious trail into the small valley. After about 0.25 mile, a sign indicates the Elliott Barker Camp trail heading left, but you'll continue going straight, walking gently uphill through a pleasant meadow. After another 0.25 mile, you'll come to a small man-made pond. Here is a delightful place to break, and if your children are small, you'll likely go no farther. Let them explore but warn them of occasional stinging nettles on the dam.

One of the things you might notice at the pond are the dragonflies. Children love watching them dart around over the water, and you might mention they're skillful and voracious hunters. A dragonfly can eat its weight in mosquitoes every half hour. Ask children how many mosquitoes that might be.

From the pond, Palo Flechado Pass is reached by hiking steadily uphill 0.75 mile through the spruce-fir forest on the old road. The forest is somewhat dense—a good place for a deep, dark woods story—and the hiking steeper than before, but the distance really isn't far, and children will feel a sense of accomplishment when they reach the pass. From there, it's all downhill.

And perhaps while you're hiking back you can tell children the story of the name Angel Fire, which belongs to the mountain, the town, and the resort just to the east. Though stories explaining this name differ in their details, most agree it began with the Moache Utes, who once lived here. One account says lightning ignited a fire on the mountain now called Angel Fire Mountain and threatened an Indian camp. Just as they were about to evacuate, the wind shifted, and a rainstorm extinguished the fire. The Indians began calling the peak "breath of spirits." When Franciscan friars encountered the legend, they Christianized the name to "breath of angels" and later to Angel Fire. Other accounts attribute the name to the reddish alpenglow on the peak at dawn and dusk, a phenomenon noted by Kit Carson, among others. When the Moache Utes were removed from the Moreno Valley in the 1870s, their legends regarding the name went with them, and not until the establishment of Angel Fire resort and ski area was interest rekindled in the poetic name.

6. El Nogal and La Vinateria Picnic Areas

Type: Dayhike
Difficulty: Easy for children
Hikable: April through November
One way: 1.5 miles
Starting elevation: 7,150 feet
High point: 7,210 feet
Maps: Carson National Forest; Taos 7.5-minute USGS quad
Hazards: None

This hike's main feature is its proximity to Taos, offering a short, easy, shaded walk near a stream as a convenient respite from the heat and crowds of summer.

The El Nogal Picnic Area is reached by driving east on Kit Carson Road from downtown Taos about 3 miles to where US 64 junctions with NM 585, at the mouth of Taos Canyon. The Carson National Forest El Nogal Picnic Area is 0.3 mile east from this junction, on the road's south side along the Rio Fernando de Taos. (The name Fernando on many features in the Taos area recalls Don Fernando de Chavez, an important landowner in the area prior to 1680.) Several national forest campgrounds can be found farther east along this road, in Taos Canyon.

In the picnic area, cross the westernmost bridge over the stream,

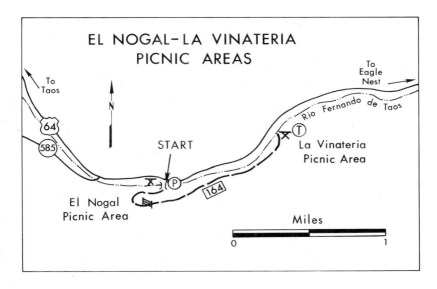

where immediately on the other side is a sign indicating Trail 164. This goes west along the creek's south side but soon leaves the stream to begin gradually ascending the slope. After about 0.25 mile this trail intersects one running level along the mountain side. Turn left, or

The spring at La Vinateria Picnic Area

east, here. Soon you'll encounter a fence and a trail descending to the left, but this just returns to the El Nogal Picnic Area.

By going straight you keep walking a level path through piñon-juniper forest. In some years, the cones of the piñon pines contain nuts whose seeds are delicious. Few people eat juniper seeds anymore, but they once were an important food for New Mexico's Native American peoples, who ground the seeds into a flour. Let children pick the gray-blue berries, crush them, and smell them. Also ask children to feel the flaking, shaggy bark, then tell them that the Ute Indians would pound this bark until it was soft and use it as diapers for their babies. The juniper tree had symbolic significance as well; Navajos carried a stick of juniper in their war dances. Point out to children that moisture availability makes the trees along the trail different from those at the campground, which include willows, box elders, and cottonwoods. Curiously, the walnut trees for which the picnic area was named—*nogal* means "walnut" in Spanish—are conspicuous by their absence. This would be a good hike on which children could make a leaf collection.

After about 1 mile you come to the La Vinateria (Spanish for "the wineshop") Picnic Area and its spring spewing from a pipe in a rock wall. Return the way you came.

7. Rio Santa Barbara

Type:	Dayhike
Difficulty:	Easy for children
Hikable:	May through October
One way:	2.25 miles
Starting elevation:	8,880 feet
High point:	9,360 feet
Maps:	Carson National Forest; Jicarita Peak 7.5-minute USGS quad
Hazards:	None

Heading high on the western slopes of the Sangre de Cristo Mountains, the three upper forks of the Rio Santa Barbara combine to form one of the most scenic mountain streams in northern New Mexico. In addition to scenery, this hike offers a rich variety of wildflowers, good fishing in the stream, an easy trail, and a pleasant

The Rio Santa Barbara

meadow for a picnic. During the summer, it's a refreshing mountain escape.

To reach the Rio Santa Barbara from NM 68 between Española and Taos, take NM 75 to Dixon, then continue on NM 75 to Peñasco. Here you'll take NM 73 southeast, continuing southeast past Rodarte on Forest Road 116 through the settlement of Llano Largo on the east

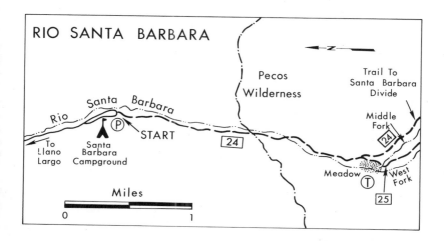

side of the Rio Santa Barbara and into the Carson National Forest, where signs will indicate the Santa Barbara Campground, about 3 miles inside the forest boundary.

The trail, 24, begins at the far south end of the Santa Barbara Campground. Its destination isn't marked, but it's easy to recognize, as it keeps the Rio Santa Barbara on the left. The outset of the trail is marked by fields of daisies and stands of aspens; the aspen leaves are magnificent in the fall. Aspen is a favorite species of almost everyone. Because it's a successional species, coming in after a fire or other disturbance, aspen groves tend to be open and sunny. Also, because aspen rarely are propagated by seeds but rather grow from the roots of neighboring trees, they often form pure stands. Sadly, the pale green bark is very soft, and many trees are defaced by people carving their initials with knives. Tell children this would be like someone giving them a tattoo against their will!

The trail is wide and easy to follow, without any side trails on which to take a wrong turn. Make a game with children about spotting different wildflower species; among those they're likely to see are aster, monkshood, yellow sneezeweed, sticky geranium, yarrow, cow parsley, and harebell. Late in the summer numerous species of mushrooms appear on the damp, decaying vegetation on the forest floor. These may look tasty, but tell children never to eat a wild mushroom.

After about 1 mile is a sign indicating the Pecos Wilderness boundary. After about 1.25 miles you reach a sign that says the junction of the middle and west forks is just a mile farther. At 1.5 miles you cross onto the east side of the Rio Santa Barbara and gently ascend the mountainside. Near the stream junction is a trail junction, marked by a sign: to the left. Trail 24 continues along the Middle Fork of the Rio Santa Barbara to the Santa Barbara Divide and eventually to Pecos Falls. Trail 25, the more heavily used trail, goes along the West Fork and leads to Truchas Lakes; total distance from the campground to the lakes is 12 miles.

But you're not going to either. Follow the lower trail, 25, downhill less than 100 yards to a pleasant meadow with views of cliffs across the valley. If you're very lucky, you might also see a mule deer. Tell children these were named for their long, mulelike ears. They're found throughout the West, but this area of the Pecos Wilderness typifies the kind of habitat they prefer. Contrary to many people's belief, deer don't graze on grass but rather browse on the edible portions of shrubs, so neither grasslands nor dense forests are their preferred habitat. Instead, they like the margins between forests and grasslands, where shrubs are both abundant and diverse. This is somewhat in contrast to the Rocky Mountain elk, also common in the Pecos Wilderness, who do spend much of their time grazing on grasses in meadows.

The meadow is a perfect place for a picnic or a break. It's a good place to relax, watch clouds, listen to the sound of the stream, feel the cool mountain air, and just experience what makes the Sangre de Cristo Mountains so special.

---

8. Chimney Rock

Type: Dayhike
Difficulty: Moderate for children
Hikable: April through November
One way: 1.5 miles
Starting elevation: 6,500 feet
High point: 7,120 feet
Map: Ghost Ranch 7.5-minute USGS quad
Hazards: Cliffs

This area is to geology what a major zoo is to animals. All along this hike are varied and dramatic rock formations, whose colors and

Chimney Rock at Ghost Ranch

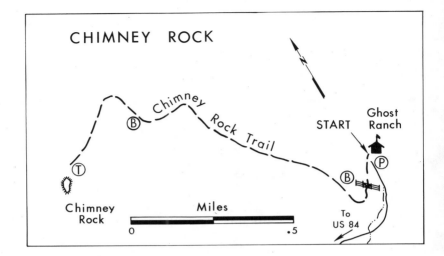

shapes have made the Ghost Ranch Conference Center among the most beautiful sites in New Mexico.

Ghost Ranch is located off US 84, about 35 miles north of Española and 6.4 miles north of the intersection with NM 96. But before exiting from US 84 onto a dirt road leading to the conference center, first drive a few miles farther northwest on US 84 to the Ghost Ranch Visitor Center, maintained by the Carson National Forest. Here you can become acquainted with the rocks, plants, and animals you'll see later. (With any luck, the only rattlesnake you'll see will be at the visitor center!) Just about 2 miles north of the visitor center on US 84 is Echo Amphitheater, a beautiful concavity carved by erosion into the red stone.

After these have whetted your appetite for the area, return to the Ghost Ranch entrance and drive 1.4 miles on good dirt road to the conference center, which is privately operated by the Presbyterian Church. Hikers must register at the office, which has maps of the grounds showing trailheads, as well as an interpretive guide to the geology of the Chimney Rock Trail.

The trail, marked by a sign, begins northwest of the office and ascends by a series of stairlike plateaus. After crossing a shallow arroyo and going through a gate, the trail reaches the first plateau by climbing a short, steep slope. Here's a good place to pause, get your wind, and begin noticing the geology around you. Perhaps children can make a game of counting how many different colors of rocks they see.

The trail here crosses a pediment, a gently sloping erosional surface, before climbing again to another relatively level plateau.

Despite a few piñons and junipers, the landscape is open, with expansive views in all directions. To the southwest is Cerro Pedernal, the chisel-shaped summit made famous by the paintings of the late Georgia O'Keeffe, whose home was nearby in Abiquiu.

Soon the trail climbs again as it ascends to the mesa top. The trail is steepest here, so take your time and become distracted by the geology—boulders perched on pillars, interbedded polychrome sedimentary layers, crevices, and alcoves. The rich red color of many of the rocks comes from traces of iron. Some of the layers were created from sediments deposited in ancient oceans; other layers are fossilized sand dunes; ask your children to see if they can tell which is which.

Finally you're at the mesa top, and from here it's a short, level walk to the trail's end at an overlook facing Chimney Rock. In all directions are breathtaking views: Abiquiu Reservoir to the southwest and beyond, the highest summits of the Jemez Mountains; Ghost Ranch to the south; polychrome cliffs to the east and north; red-banded mesas to the west. But don't let children stray too close to the edge; the cliff here is sheer.

9. Kitchen Mesa

Type: Dayhike
Difficulty: Moderate to difficult for children
Hikable: April through November
One way: 3 miles
Starting elevation: 6,500 feet
High point: 7,077 feet
Map: Ghost Ranch 7.5-minute USGS quad
Hazards: Steep drop-offs

For children and adults who are strong hikers with a sense of adventure, this hike from the Ghost Ranch Conference Center will amply repay their efforts. The scenery is spectacular, the landforms are interesting, and the hiking can be exciting.

Kitchen Mesa is the dramatic bluff whose vertical cliffs overlook the center to the northeast. After registering at the center's main office (for directions to Ghost Ranch, see Chimney Rock hike 8), walk northeast on the main road back into the canyon's mouth. En route

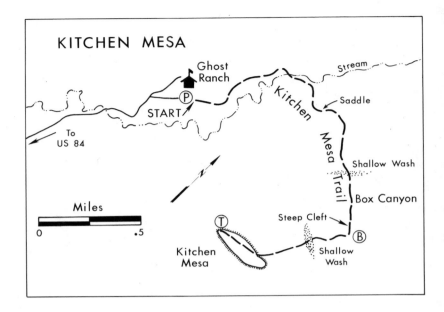

you'll pass several huge cottonwood trees that local legend says served as gallows trees for cattle rustlers. This might be a good time to tell children about how Ghost Ranch got its name. The canyon was settled near the end of the 19th century by the Archuleta family, who built a stockade of cedar poles that came to be known as the Ghost House. A girl brought up in this house said she always believed the canyon was inhabited by evil spirits, or *brujos*, including some known as "earth babies"—6 feet tall with red hair— as well as a winged cow.

As you enter the canyon's mouth, signs point the way to the Kitchen Mesa Trail. Just beyond a gate closing the road to vehicles, near the turnoff to Casitas, the Kitchen Mesa Trail branches from the road and crosses the shallow stream. Sagebrush is abundant here; tell children to crush the leaves between their fingers and savor the strong scent.

The trail briefly parallels the stream and then heads southeast, crossing over a small red-earth saddle to enter the mouth of a box canyon. As the trail follows a relatively level course into the box canyon, it is flanked on both sides by dramatic red and tan sandstone cliffs. Here as elsewhere in the Ghost Ranch area, geology is dramatically exposed. The cliffs of Kitchen Mesa are composed mainly of Entrada sandstone, formed in a sand dune desert 168 million to 166 million years ago. They're capped by a layer of gypsum, formed in a lake or ocean bay 166 million to 165 million years ago.

Nearing the back of the canyon, the trail crosses a shallow wash to the canyon's northeast side, where it begins ascending the slope. As you climb you'll wonder how you're going to get up the headwall looming ahead, and indeed, as you approach the top, you'll have to scramble about 25 feet up a steep cleft not visible from below. Adults may grumble, but children will enjoy the adventure.

Above the cleft is a good place to catch your breath and take a break. When you resume hiking, you'll turn south, cross a shallow wash, and then ascend some sandstone ledges before finally coming out on the mesa's level top. The trail now turns northwest, and the hiking is easy and interesting.

This bluff is an unusual mixture of gypsum and calcite, and sometimes the ground glistens with crystals; children can collect them, but they're very fragile. And water dissolving minerals has created intriguing crevices and formations. Farther along the bluff, vegetation eventually disappears almost entirely from this mineralized soil, and as you approach the end of the bluff, overlooking Ghost Ranch, you're walking over a surface reminiscent of a beach or sand dunes. This bluff is fun to explore, and the views here are spectacular, but keep children away from the edge, as the drop-offs are sheer. And avoid disturbing the delicate crust that's formed to protect the soil from erosion. Return the way you came.

The cliffs of Kitchen Mesa overlooking the grounds of Ghost Ranch

Santa Fe Area

Enjoying the mist behind the Rio en Medio waterfall

10. Rio en Medio Waterfall

Type: Dayhike
Difficulty: Easy for children
Hikable: April through November
One way: 2 miles
Starting elevation: 7,170 feet
High point: 8,150 feet
Maps: Santa Fe National Forest;
Tesuque and Aspen Basin
7.5-minute USGS quads
Hazards: Occasional poison ivy

This is a pleasant little expedition from Santa Fe, taking you on a drive through some interesting villages, through the scenic foothills of the Sangre de Cristo Mountains, then to a relatively short and easy hike along a stream in the woods, with the goal of reaching an impressive waterfall.

To reach the trailhead from the village of Tesuque north of Santa Fe, drive north on the main paved road in the village to where paved NM 592 branches right. Drive east and north on this for 3.8 miles to where the pavement ends in the diffuse community of Rio en Medio, named for the stream of that name issuing from the mountains here.

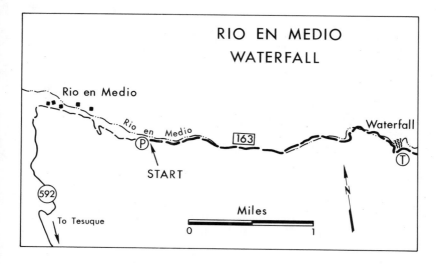

RIO EN MEDIO
WATERFALL

Rio en Medio

Rio en Medio

Waterfall

163

START

592

To Tesuque

Miles

N

0   1

At the end of the pavement, continue on the good dirt road 0.8 mile to a small parking area. The road appears to continue but in fact ends soon after the parking area. There, where the road is closed to block access to private land, a trail branches right and is marked by a sign indicating Trail 163.

Trail 163 hugs the south hillside, snaking through dense vegetation that often includes poison ivy, that ubiquitous resident in moist, lower canyons in New Mexico. Here's a good opportunity to challenge children to see if they can spot the plant with the shiny leaves in groups of three. After about 0.25 mile, the trail returns to the valley floor and for the rest of the hike follows the stream, crossing it several times. The trail often is poorly marked, with numerous alternate paths, but all of them follow the stream, all are relatively level, and all lead eventually to the waterfall. In summer and fall, the stream crossings pose few problems—beyond wet feet—for parties with children, but the water is much higher in the spring, when the creek is swollen by meltwater from the upper slopes of the mountains. This is a hike where walking sticks are much appreciated for the stability they provide.

The waterfall is reached where the trail begins a steep, rocky ascent and is heard before it's seen. From the top of the rocks you can peer down to the waterfall—keep children away from the edge. The fall is best seen from its base, but unfortunately this can be very difficult to reach and can involve wading in the stream. It's worth it, however, and adventuresome children in particular would enjoy exploring the small, mossy hollow behind the fall. The top of the rocks also is a natural place to break or turn around.

Above the fall the trail begins to climb, the vegetation changes from foothills to montane, and the Rio en Medio descends in a series of rocky cascades. The trail eventually ends at the Santa Fe Ski Area, but most parties with children will go no farther than the waterfall.

As you hike back to your car, you might think about this "river" that you're following. Three *rios*, or rivers, rise high in the Sangre de Cristo Mountains behind Santa Fe and flow west: the Rio Nambe to the north, the Rio Chupadero to the south, and this "river in the middle," for that is what the Spanish Rio en Medio means in English. Persons from the East, accustomed to rivers like the Mississippi and the Potomac, tend to scoff at such rivers as this, which during some seasons a long-legged person could leap across. But the Rio en Medio seems to know its worth in this arid land, for it is energetic and aggressive as it rushes down the Sangre de Cristo slopes, and without these rivers, settlement of much of New Mexico would have been impossible. At least the Rio en Medio has water all year long; one river in southwestern New Mexico, the lower Mimbres River, has had water flowing in it only once in 50 years.

11. Chamisa Trail

Type: Dayhike
Difficulty: Moderate for children
Hikable: April through November
One way: 2.25 miles
Starting elevation: 7,810 feet
High point: 8,500 feet
Maps: Santa Fe National Forest;
Aspen Basin and McClure
Reservoir 7.5-minute USGS
quads
Hazards: None

When the crowds and heat of downtown Santa Fe become over-whelming, make a quick escape on this relatively short and easy, shaded trail to a secluded, wildflower-filled meadow along a cool mountain stream.

To reach the Chamisa Trail from the Plaza in Santa Fe, go north on Washington Street six blocks, past the huge pink Scottish Rite

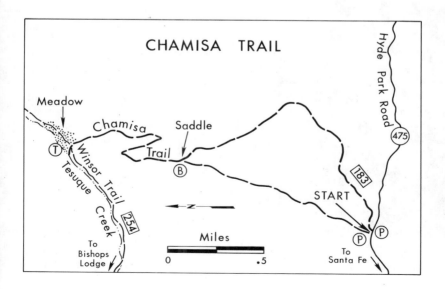

Temple, then turn right onto Artist Road, where a sign points to Hyde Memorial State Park and the Santa Fe Ski Area. Drive east on Artist Road, which becomes Hyde Park Road, NM 475, for 5.6 miles to where a canyon enters from the north. Parking is available on both sides of the road. On the east side of the north parking area is a sign labelling Trail 183. Another trail, unmarked but plainly visible, goes directly up the canyon through the dusty-green chamisas for which the trail was named. This alternate trail follows the watercourse and is wet in the spring, but it is more direct than Trail 183, which it joins at a saddle after 1 mile.

As you begin hiking, take a moment to mention the chamisas to your children. Chamisa is the name Hispanic New Mexicans use for several varieties of the shrub known to English speakers as rabbit-brush. Chamisa is especially common in northern New Mexico. In the fall, especially around Santa Fe, roadsides, arroyos, and canyons often are golden with its flowers, and the air is heavy with the thick, sweet scent that reminds me of honey. Rural people for centuries have used the shrub's easily ignited wood as kindling, and long before the Spaniards arrived the Indians used the slender, flexible branches, stripped of bark, for basket making.

Trail 183 goes east for a few hundred feet, then turns north, climbing steadily through pleasant forest, with views into the canyon below. After 1.25 miles you'll reach a saddle, where the other trail enters from the left. Here's a good place to catch your breath and enjoy the mountain air. Several species of conifers grow along the trail, and children may want to collect their cones, especially the giant cones, some almost a foot long, of the limber pine. In the fall, in some years, the piñon pines produce edible nuts in their cones.

From the saddle the Chamisa Trail descends, continuing in a generally northerly direction.

Sampling piñon nuts on the Chamisa Trail

Occasionally it follows a dry streambed, wet in the spring, and the footing sometimes is rocky. After 1 mile, however, the trail levels out, and you find yourself at the lower edge of a large, pleasant meadow on Tesuque Creek. Here the Chamisa Trail ends at its junction with the Winsor Trail 254, marked by a sign that says Bishops Lodge is 3.75 miles downstream, while upstream the ski area is 6.5 miles.

Enjoy the meadow; take a break in the soft grass beneath one of the large ponderosa pines or beside the conspicuous granite boulder. Let your children explore Tesuque Creek; they'll like seeing the dams made by beavers. Then stroll up the valley along the Winsor Trail before returning the way you came. The swelter of downtown Santa Fe will seem delightfully remote.

12. Borrego Trail

Type: Dayhike
Difficulty: Moderate for children
Hikable: April through October
One way: 1.5 miles or a 4-mile loop
Starting elevation: 8,875 feet
High point: 8,880 feet
Maps: Santa Fe National Forest;
Aspen Basin and McClure
Reservoir 7.5-minute USGS
quads
Hazards: None

In the Sangre de Cristo Mountains, nature is often quick to forget the ephemera of human affairs. For example, on the Borrego Trail east of Santa Fe only the name survives as a clue that a century ago the trail was loud with the baaing of hundreds of sheep, the exhortation of shepherds, and the barking of dogs pursuing strays.

For the Spanish, *borrego* means sheep, and once this trail was part of the route followed by sheep herders driving their flocks from the high pastures of the Sangre de Cristo Mountains to market in Santa Fe. The sheep would have trampled a broad swath through the forest undergrowth and consumed all edible vegetation.

Today, aster, scarlet gilia, clover, and even shy pipsissewa bloom unthreatened along the trail, which is no longer a sheep route but

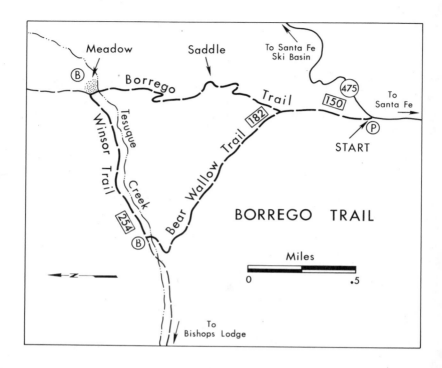

a hiking trail. Indeed, it's among the most popular in the southern Sangre de Cristos—and for good reasons. It's convenient to Santa Fe, it's very easy to follow, and it offers a refreshing escape from the midsummer heat.

The Borrego trailhead is reached from Santa Fe by taking Washington Avenue north from the Plaza, past the huge pink Scottish Rite Temple, to Artist Road, where a sign points to Hyde Memorial State Park and Santa Fe Ski Area. Santa Fe National Forest campgrounds are nearby, as well as at the ski area. This road, NM 475, goes east and north into the mountains, passing through the state park, to arrive after 8.5 miles at the trailhead on the left side of the road, marked by a Santa Fe National Forest sign.

From the trailhead, the Borrego Trail 150 descends into a shaded forest of firs, aspens, and ponderosa pines. After 0.5 mile, the trail branches. The left fork, leading slightly downhill, is the Bear Wallow Trail 182. This connects after 1 mile with Tesuque Creek and the Winsor Trail 254. Follow the Winsor Trail uphill and along the stream for 1.5 miles to its junction with the Borrego Trail at a meadow. It's another mile over the Borrego Trail back to the junction. The entire round-trip loop is only 4 miles.

But an even easier route is to continue on the Borrego Trail by taking the right fork at the Bear Wallow Trail junction. This meanders through the forest, ascends a small saddle, and then drops down the other side to enter a pleasant meadow just after crossing Tesuque Creek.

The Borrego Trail is especially appropriate for children or persons just wanting a leisurely stroll in the woods. When Albuquerque and Santa Fe are sweltering, the Borrego Trail is delightfully cool. And though towering trees shade virtually all the trail, the undergrowth is lush and diverse. In midsummer as many as twenty-five wildflower species bloom along the trail, including harebell, monkshood, bee balm, and vervain. My family often makes a game out of counting how many

Crossing Tesuque Creek requires negotiating a fallen log.

species we can spot; variations of the game can include awarding bonus points for certain kinds of flowers, such as blue ones or ones with a pleasing scent.

The meadow is an obvious stopping point and ideal for picnics. Children can explore along the stream, though being careful of occasional stinging nettle. Tesuque Creek rises high in the Sangre de Cristo Mountains above 10,000 feet; its waters are clear and cold. Don't let children stray out of sight of the meadow, however, as the topography can be confusing.

As you hike back, ask your children to imagine what it might have been like, 100 years ago, to walk here surrounded by noisy, smelly sheep and know that Santa Fe and a soft bed were not minutes but a whole day away.

13. Winsor Trail to Puerto Nambe

Type: Dayhike or backpack
Difficulty: Moderate to difficult for children
Hikable: June through September
One way: 4 miles
Starting elevation: 10,280 feet
High point: 11,000 feet
Maps: Santa Fe National Forest; Aspen Basin 7.5-minute USGS quad
Hazards: None

Here is the New Mexico high country most easily accessible from Santa Fe, the lush, flower-dappled meadows, intensely beautiful during their brief season against the backdrop of the southern Sangre de Cristo Mountains, the most southerly of the Rocky Mountain chain. It's a realm of cloud-scraping peaks, subalpine tarns, quaking aspen forests—and sudden storms and steep slopes. The Winsor Trail has all of these.

The trailhead is reached from the Santa Fe Plaza by going north on Washington Street six blocks, past the huge pink Scottish Rite Temple, then turning right onto Artist Road, where a sign points to the Santa Fe Ski Area, 15 miles. At the ski area the Winsor Trail

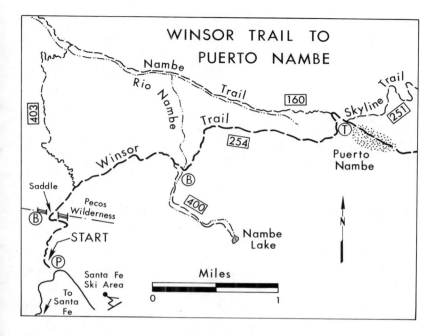

254 starts on the southwest side of the parking area and is marked by a sign.

The trail begins with a steep, relentless climb for 0.5 mile to the Pecos Wilderness Boundary at a saddle marked by a fence with a pass-through. This is a good spot to break and adjust equipment. Canadian jays frequent this spot and with little encouragement will eat crumbs from hikers' hands, something children delight in. This aggressive eagerness to eat human food has earned these birds the common name "camp robbers." Feeding them should not be encouraged but sometimes is hard to resist.

From the saddle the trail descends 0.4 mile to the junction with Trail 403, which leads steeply downhill 1.8 miles to Rio Nambe. The Winsor Trail continues gently downhill along the upper slopes for another 0.7 mile until it reaches Nambe Creek, coming from Nambe Lake far above. Here is another natural point at which to break or turn around if you just want a pleasant dayhike. Children might want to play or wade in the creek, but its waters are very cold. The poorly signed but easy to follow Trail 400 follows the creek 1.5 miles to Nambe Lake, a scenic, shallow pond—no fish—at the foot of Lake Peak. This trail, however, is very steep and will seem much longer than its relatively short distance. Because of human pressure, camping is not permitted in the lake basin.

A brook feeding Nambe Lake in the Sangre de Cristo Mountains

From Nambe Creek, the Winsor Trail continues northeast through pleasant aspen-spruce-fir forest and small meadows, climbing slightly. Here is another sign saying Puerto Nambe is only 0.75 mile away, but it will seem farther as, after crossing intermittent streams, the Winsor Trail begins a somewhat steep ascent, rewarding the effort with spectacular views of 12,622-foot Santa Fe Baldy to the north.

This might be a good time to distract your children by talking about the name of the mountains they're in—Sangre de Cristo. It's Spanish and means "blood of Christ." Numerous apocryphal legends explain the name, the most common being that a priest, mortally wounded in the Pueblo Revolt of 1680, begged God for a sign; looking east he beheld these mountains, blood-red in the evening light, and exclaimed, "Sangre de Cristo!" It's an appealing story, but the name actually dates only from the early 1800s and likely is associated with the Penitente religious group and their devotion to the Passion and

Death of Christ. Penitente Peak, at 12,249 feet, dominates the skyline just south of Puerto Nambe. Before the nineteenth century, these mountains were called La Sierra Madre, "the mother mountains," or simply La Sierra.

Finally, after about 2.4 miles from Nambe Creek, you reach Puerto Nambe, a grassy meadow between Lake Peak and Penitente Peak to the south and Santa Fe Baldy to the north. This meadow is a deservedly popular camping spot for hikers in the Pecos Wilderness, and campers are likely to see backpackers, horseback riders, and even parties with llamas.

From here the Skyline Trail 251 leaves the Winsor Trail and ascends northeasterly to a saddle before descending to Lake Katherine. This also is the route for climbing Santa Fe Baldy, a not-too-difficult hike in good weather; simply ascend the ridge to your left from the saddle.

A word of caution if you plan on hiking here during New Mexico's "monsoon season," late July through early September: Be prepared for afternoon rain, sometimes heavy, and accompanying lightning. At this elevation, thunderstorms can arise suddenly, and an electrical storm can be a terrifying and dangerous experience. Watch the weather closely. A good lesson to teach your children is that when it comes to lightning, discretion is indeed the better part of valor, and a hasty retreat is nothing to be ashamed of.

14. El Temporal Nature Trail and Bear Canyon

Type: Dayhike
Difficulty: Easy for children
Hikable: Year-round
One way: 1 mile
Starting elevation: 7,375 feet
High point: 8,100 feet
Map: Santa Fe 7.5-minute USGS quad
Hazards: None

For Santa Fe visitors who want to escape to nature for a couple of hours, this is a delightful little hike, especially in the spring. And

BEAR CANYON TRAIL

Santa Fe River

(P)

Meadow

Randall Davey
Audubon Center

Upper Canyon Road

Nature
Trail

START

Bear Canyon Trail

To
Santa Fe

N

Miles

0   .25

(T)

because it's based at the Randall Davey Audubon Center, it's a good opportunity to introduce children to some of northern New Mexico's birds.

The center is reached by driving east on Upper Canyon Road from Camino Cabra (Spanish for "goat road") to where the pavement ends at 1.3 miles. From here drive on dirt another 0.5 mile to the Randall Davey Audubon Center, marked by signs. Admission to the grounds is $1, and a little interpretive guide to the El Temporal Nature Trail is 50 cents. This trail is a 0.5-mile loop around a meadow with scattered piñon and juniper trees; the trail crosses a historic acequia, or water ditch. While interesting, the meadow is exposed and is at its best in cooler weather.

One of the main features of the El Temporal Trail is the Acequia del Llano, or "ditch of the plain." These acequias are the traditional irrigation systems of New Mexico and have been important not only for agriculture but also for community life, as the annual cleaning of the acequia of unwanted vegetation, organized by the mayordomo, or ditch boss, is an important community event. The main acequia in a region, the trunk from which others branch, is called the acequia madre. The Acequia del Llano brings water to residents of Upper Canyon Road.

At the meadow's southeast end, another trail diverges from the El Temporal Trail and leads into a canyon. This trail is not marked and the canyon has no formal name, but the trail and the canyon are easy to find, and the people at the Audubon center call it Bear Canyon. Maybe your children can imagine stories to explain the name, or perhaps they can think up their own names for this canyon.

This trail follows the watercourse up Bear Canyon through shady ponderosa forest. By midsummer the streambed is dry, but in the spring and early summer a pleasant little stream is flowing, a good place to wade and cool hot feet. The trail sometimes is obscure, but it never strays far from the streambed, so keep close to that and you'll not get lost. After about 1 mile, the trail becomes steeper, rockier, and drier, quickly losing appeal for most hikers. Children will like the lower, moister stretches better, and as the Audubon center people put it, all trails are interesting to children accompanied by observant adults willing to talk and listen.

The El Temporal Trail and nearby Bear Canyon are excellent places to look for birds, as the areas are interfaces between plant communities, where the ecological diversity results in more abundant food sources for birds. When you leave the nature center to hike, perhaps your party can do a bird count, keeping track of how many kinds you see. Some species you might encounter are nuthatches, chickadees, Steller's jays, juncos, and flickers. Dusty-blue piñon jays often form large flocks; they were named for their fondness for piñon nuts.

The tiny creek in Bear Canyon

When you return from your hike, take your children to the Randall Davey Audubon Center, where exhibits and staff can help identify some of the plants and wildlife you saw. The site has historic as well as natural significance, for here in 1847 the U.S. Army built the first sawmill in New Mexico Territory. From 1892 to 1920, Candelario Martinez raised crops and tended orchards here. Then in 1920 the property was sold to artist Randall Davey. It's a facet of Santa Fe's cultural and natural history that most tourists on the Plaza miss.

15. Mora Flats

Type: Dayhike or backpack
Difficulty: Easy to moderate for children
Hikable: May through October
One way: 3 miles
Starting elevation: 9,350 feet
High point: 9,800 feet
Maps: Pecos Wilderness, Santa Fe National Forest, and Carson National Forest; Elk Mountain 7.5-minute USGS quad
Hazards: None

This part of the Pecos Wilderness deservedly is among the most popular hiking and backpacking regions in New Mexico, and for people with children Mora Flats deservedly is among the most popular destinations. The trail is relatively short, the hiking easy, the scenery beautiful, and the campsites appealing. What's more, driving to the trailhead takes you by some of New Mexico's most significant historic sites.

To reach the trailhead, drive via Interstate 25 to the village of Pecos. If you're driving from Santa Fe, take the exit marked Glorieta-Pecos and go southeast on NM 50. This route parallels the old Santa Fe Trail and takes you past the site of the Glorieta Battlefield, a key battle of the Civil War, where on March 8, 1862, Union forces decisively defeated Confederate troops and doomed the Southern cause in New Mexico. If you're driving from the east on Interstate 25, take the Rowe exit and drive northwest on NM 50. Here you'll go past Pecos National Monument, preserving the ruins of the abandoned Towa

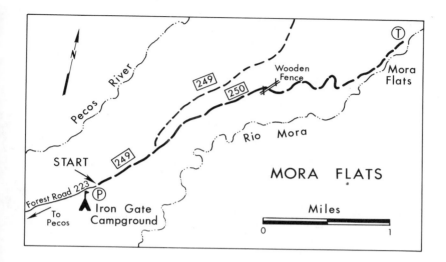

Indian pueblo that 400 years ago likely was the largest settlement in what is now the United States. The name Pecos sounds like a Spanish word, but in fact it is a corruption of a Keresan Indian word meaning "place where there is water." The Indians who lived at the pueblo are said to have called it Cicuye.

Drive on NM 50 into the village of Pecos until its intersection with NM 63, which you'll follow as it parallels the Pecos River into the Santa Fe National Forest. At 18.5 miles from the intersection with NM 50, a dirt road, Forest Road 223, branches right to the national forest Iron Gate Campground. This road is steep and rough but with care can be negotiated by most cars. The road winds through an area of summer homes, with numerous side roads, but the main route is marked and fairly apparent. After 4.4 miles you reach Iron Gate Campground.

Returning from Mora Flats

(There are other national forest campgrounds in the area, especially along the Pecos River between Pecos and Cowles, but all campgrounds tend to be crowded in the summer, especially on weekends.)

Iron Gate Campground is at the edge of the 223,667-acre Pecos Wilderness, and most of your hiking will be within the wilderness. This was created in 1933 to preserve the wildlands surrounding the headwaters of the Pecos River, for which it was named.

The trailhead for Mora Flats is at the campground's northeast end. You'll start by hiking Trail 249, which goes to Hamilton Mesa, though Mora Flats also is marked by a sign here. Trail 249 goes gently uphill through pleasant spruce-fir forest for 0.25 mile until it reaches a ridge overlooking the canyon of the Rio Mora far below. After another 0.75 mile or less, you reach the intersection with Trail 250, branching right and leading to Mora Flats.

Trail 250 descends very gradually. As you hike you'll pass through stands of ponderosa pine or, more commonly, beautiful aspen groves interspersed with meadows. You might take a break with your children in one of these groves and talk to them about the trees here. These are the famous quaking, or trembling, aspens of the West. Note how their leaves flutter or quake in the wind, resulting in the nickname "quakies." To help children understand how this happens, have them take a leaf and notice how the leaf stalk is flattened at right angles to the leaf. In the fall in New Mexico, the quaking aspen leaves turn a brilliant shimmering gold, and where aspens cover whole mountainsides the effect is spectacular.

Early in the season wild iris is abundant in the meadows and aspen groves; their alternative name is blue flag. Other flowers common along the trail are golden pea, wild rose, shrubby cinquefoil, penstemon, and aster. This is a good time to play a flower game, such as the one in which everyone looks for the tallest flower, the shortest, the most showy, the most fragrant, and so on. There usually are enough flowers along this trail and at the flats to keep children interested for the entire hike.

After about a mile on Trail 250 you pass through a wooden fence, and soon after you begin to see far below the meadows of Mora Flats. The trail descends, usually gently, until about 0.5 mile from the meadow a few brief switchbacks take you onto the valley floor.

Here you enter a conifer grove through which flow the clear waters of the Rio Mora. Several excellent campsites are obvious here. If you choose to spend the night, try to pick one of these campsites rather than create a new one—and reuse existing fire rings. This area receives heavy use, and campers have an obligation to minimize their impact.

Take time to explore the meadows. One plant you'll notice is yellow-blossomed shrubby cinquefoil. Its name means "five leaves," and children can easily see why. Harebells also are abundant, and, early in the season, so is blue columbine. If you're lucky enough to find these, take a moment to tell children about the columbine's name. The genus is *Aquilegia*, from *aquila*, the Latin word for "eagle," because the spurs of the flower's petals are said to resemble an eagle's claws. The common name, columbine, comes from another Latin word, *columba*, meaning "dove," because the petals are thought to look like a circular cluster of doves.

Return the way you came. You'll likely find the trip will go quickly as you discover why this area is so beloved among New Mexico hikers.

16. Cave Creek

Type:	Dayhike or short backpack
Difficulty:	Easy to moderate for children
Hikable:	May through October
One way:	2.5 miles
Starting elevation:	8,350 feet
High point:	8,600 feet
Maps:	Pecos Wilderness, Santa Fe National Forest, and Carson National Forest; Cowles 7.5-minute USGS quad
Hazards:	None

Here's a child-sized adventure in the Pecos Wilderness, an easy, pleasant hike to a stream that plunges into a cave and then emerges again. It's not Carlsbad Caverns, but kids will be impressed, and it's a great excuse for a drive along the scenic and historic Pecos River.

To reach the trailhead, drive on NM 50 through the village of Pecos to the intersection with NM 63, which you'll follow as it parallels the Pecos River into the Santa Fe National Forest. At 14 miles you'll reach the tiny settlement of Terrero, where food, gas, and supplies are available. Just above Terrero are the remains of mining operations; until mining dwindled in the 1930s, as many as 3,000 people lived here. Continue on the paved road north from Terrero toward the summer-home area of Cowles, reached at 19.6 miles from Pecos. In Cowles, just past the small lake on the west, the road turns left to

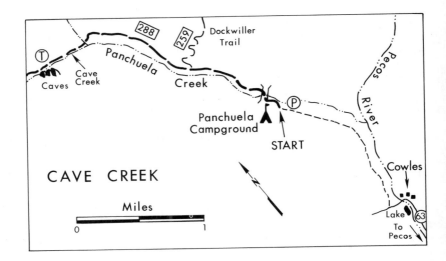

Dockwiller Trail

Panchuela Creek

Cave Creek

Caves

Panchuela Campground

START

CAVE CREEK

Miles

0   1

Pecos River

Cowles

Lake

To Pecos

cross the Pecos River. After just 0.1 mile the road to the national forest Panchuela Campground branches sharply to the right and uphill. During some seasons, the campground and the road to it are closed— if so, consider walking along the road; the walking is easy and scenic. Drive or walk on this about 1 mile to the campground. Parking for wilderness hikers is just before the campground itself.

From the Panchuela parking area, walk into the campground, then cross the small but vigorous Panchuela Creek over a small bridge. Here the trail follows the creek briefly before making a short climb above the stream, where the gradient again becomes gentle. From here until the caves, the hiking is easy as the trail winds through pleasant, flower-filled meadows and forests of ponderosa pine, Douglas fir, spruce, and aspen.

As you hike, ask children to notice the dark, bristly clusters in the tops of many conifers, conspicuously denser than the surrounding pine needles. This is mistletoe (yes, the same as that used at Christmas), a common parasite of conifers throughout the West. The mistletoe taps into the tree's food delivery system, taking water and nutrients, yet provides nothing in return for the tree.

As your children hike, ask them to notice also the gray-green moss dangling from many tree branches. This moss is called old man's beard (ask children to suggest their names for this scraggly moss). It uses the tree to provide a place from which it can hang and absorb moisture, but it asks nothing else of the tree, and the relationship is rather benign for both species.

At the north end of a meadow, you'll notice a trail joining your trail from the left. This trail, not labeled, is simply an alternate route back to the campground. Soon, within the first mile, the Dockwiller Trail 259 will branch right and uphill, but you'll take the left fork, Trail 288, the Cave Creek Trail. This trail follows a generally level or slightly downhill gradient through pleasant meadows and spruce-fir forest. Children can learn to tell the difference between these two easily confused trees by remembering that the needles of fir, beginning with *f*, are *flat* and *flexible*, whereas the needles of spruce, beginning with *s*, are *square* and *spiky*.

In late summer and early fall, the meadows here are filled with lavender asters. The name comes from the Greek word for "star," and legend says Asteria, the Greek goddess of stars, looked down upon the earth and, saddened at seeing no stars there, began to cry. Where her tears fell, these flowers sprouted. She must have wept copiously, because asters are among the most common and widely distributed wildflowers in North America.

About 1.5 miles from the campground, the trail dips to cross Panchuela Creek. Just across the stream is a pleasant little clearing that would make a good campsite, though you'd have little privacy, as Pecos Wilderness trails such as this are heavily used during the summer. At this crossing Cave Creek joins Panchuela Creek, and the Cave Creek Trail follows Cave Creek on its north side. As you and the children hike, suggest making a game out of listening to the creek. In slightly less than 0.5 mile you'll notice the creek suddenly becomes quiet, and if you look you'll find its flow dramatically reduced. The caves are near. You'll encounter the first cave just about 0.5 mile up the trail from Panchuela Creek, marked only by a faint spur trail leading left toward the stream, but less than 100 yards farther along the trail are the three main caves. You'll be alerted to their presence by suddenly hearing the creek again.

The three main caves are close together on the creek's south side; when you approach them you'll see the stream plunging down into one of them. The caves are all connected. I don't recommend going into the caves beyond their entrances. If your children do wish to explore farther, make sure they're accompanied by an adult with several reliable sources of light.

As you hike back, listen for the resumption of the creek noise about 200 yards downstream from the caves, then go to the stream to watch it issuing from the rocks.

Jemez Mountains

Tent Rocks (Photo: Joel Pearson)

17. Tsankawi Ruins

Type: Dayhike
Difficulty: Easy for children
Hikable: March through November
One way: 0.75 mile
Starting elevation: 6,500 feet
High point: 6,680 feet
Map: White Rock 7.5-minute USGS quad
Hazards: Steep drop-offs

After more than 400 years, Kokopelli still plays his flute at the ruins of Tsankawi south of Los Alamos. There, on a weathered face of soft volcanic tuff, the petroglyph of the sacred hunchbacked flute player of the Pueblo Indians can still be seen, but each year it grows more indistinct. And each year Kokopelli becomes a more appropriate symbol for the ruins themselves.

In recent years, the National Park Service, which administers the site as part of Bandelier National Monument, closed Tsankawi to visitors because of increasing vandalism and plundering of artifacts. Later it was reopened to the public, but its long-term future is in doubt. If you have a chance to hike here, do so—but hike gently.

And as you walk this trail, sometimes worn a foot deep in the soft volcanic tuff of this scenic mesa, remind your children that some of the Indian feet that wore these grooves belonged to children much like them.

Perhaps more than anywhere else, Tsankawi ruins are an excellent introduction to the ancient people who once inhabited the Pajarito Plateau and whose descendants now live in the pueblos along the Rio Grande.

Just why they chose this site is a mystery. Certainly the Indians would have enjoyed spectacular scenery. To the east, across the Rio Grande Valley, are the high peaks of the Sangre de Cristo Mountains. To the west and north are the major Jemez summits, including Chicoma, the highest, sacred to the Tewas. To the south are the serrated Sandia Mountains.

But scenery is a poor substitute for water, which is lacking on the mesa (be sure to take some). Though mesa-top reservoirs would have held occasional rainwater, these would have been inadequate

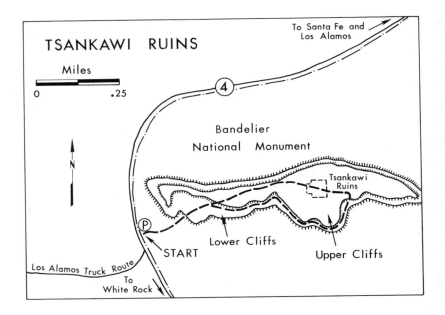

during dry seasons, and the nearest reliable water sources are far away. And while the cliffs ringing the mesa are excellent defensively, archaeologists say they've found no evidence of warfare.

The mesa was first settled in the late 1100s and inhabited about 400 years. Residents at the modern Tewa pueblo of San Ildefonso say their ancestors lived at Tsankawi; the name comes from Tewa words meaning "village between two canyons, at the clump of sharp, round cacti." In the late 1500s, after the Spaniards had arrived, the pueblo inexplicably was abandoned, as were many villages on the Pajarito Plateau.

To reach the site from Santa Fe, take US 84-285 north 10 miles to Pojoaque, then drive west toward Los Alamos on NM 502 for 10 miles to the junction with NM 4. Drive southwest on NM 4 about 1 mile; the Tsankawi Ruins parking area is on the left side of the road and is marked. The National Park Service charges an entry fee and sells trail guides.

This ready access is part of Tsankawi's appeal, especially for families, because children crawling in and out of the caves, clambering up and down the wooden ladders, running along the narrow ledges, and shouting to each other across the mesa top make it easier to visualize the site when it was inhabited by Indian families centuries ago.

The trail, which is a loop beginning at the parking lot, is mostly level, but some sections involve climbing pole ladders and ascending narrow crevices—just as the ancient Indians did. Children will love these features. The trail takes you first onto the mesa's top. Here are the ruins of a small village, now mostly mounds of rubble but with the remains of walls still visible. The views from here are spectacular.

From the mesa top you descend via a ladder to the shelf surrounding most of the mesa. In the soft stone—compressed volcanic ash—are grottoes and caves. Some of these were enlarged and shaped by the ancient residents into rooms for dwelling and storage. Children delight in crawling in and out of these. As they explore, remind them that the smoke-blackened ceilings show that people once spent cold winter nights here.

Reminders of the Indians are everywhere—potsherds (don't remove them), ruined walls, footworn paths, caves carved in the soft stone, and petroglyphs. The Kokopelli petroglyph is on the mesa's south side, near the end of the trail, but it's very faint and difficult to see.

And if your children ask to remove their shoes to feel the soft stone against their bare feet, consider joining them. Experiencing the past is what Tsankawi is all about.

---

18. Alcove House (Ceremonial Cave) and Cañon de los Frijoles

Type:	Dayhike
Difficulty:	Easy for children
Hikable:	Year-round
One way:	1.25 miles, including the Ruins Trail
Starting elevation:	6,066 feet
High point:	About 6,450 feet
Map:	Frijoles 7.5-minute USGS quad
Hazards:	Cliffs at the cave

It's easy to see why this canyon appealed to the Pueblo Indians who lived here 500 years ago. The cool, lush vegetation along the perennial stream in the narrow Cañon de los Frijoles would have been in dramatic contrast to the exposed, arid mesas above. And perhaps the Indian children also delighted in the grottoes and caves dotting the

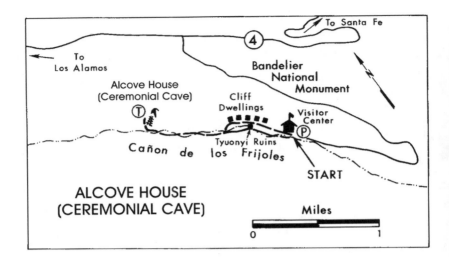

To Santa Fe

To
Los Alamos

Bandelier
National
Monument

Alcove House
(Ceremonial Cave)

Cliff
Dwellings

Visitor
Center

Tyuonyi Ruins

Cañon de los Frijoles

START

ALCOVE HOUSE
(CEREMONIAL CAVE)

Miles

0   1

Descending a pole ladder from Alcove House (Ceremonial Cave).

soft volcanic tuff of the canyon's walls like holes in a sea-sponge.

Frijoles is Spanish and means "beans." The canyon was named for the beans the Indians grew here. Other plants they cultivated for food were squash, corn, and amaranth.

Cañon de los Frijoles had other significance for the Indians as well. The inhabitants of Cochiti Pueblo to the south say their ancestors once lived here. The Keresan name of the main ruin, Tyuonyi, means "place of the treaty" in English, referring to a pact between the Keresan Indians to the south and the Tewa Indians to the north. Indeed, archaeologists have determined that the canyon marks the boundary between Keres and Tewa territories. The Tewas call the ruin *Puqwige'onwikeji*, "old pueblo where the bottoms of the pottery vessels were smoothed thin."

In modern times this canyon has become the main attraction of Bandelier National Monument, named for Adolph F. Bandelier (1840–1914). This ethnologist and historian conducted pioneering research throughout the Pajarito Plateau, where hundreds of archaeological sites reveal that once this was an area of dense settlement. One of the most accessible sites is at Tsankawi, hike 17.

Bandelier National Monument is reached from Santa Fe by driving north on US 84-285 to Pojoaque, then west on NM 502 and south on NM 4. Parking, rest rooms, food, and information are available at the visitor center, where the hike up Cañon de los Frijoles begins.

Several trails lead up the canyon from the visitor center, but adults and children likely will want to start by exploring the cliff dwellings at the base of the canyon's east wall. The trail to these leads you past the ruins of Tyuonyi, a village and ceremonial site just 0.25 mile north of the center.

The cliff dwellings are visible from Tyuonyi, and the Ruins Trail along the cliff's base takes you by them. Portions of the trail are paved and accessible to wheelchairs and strollers. Children will love exploring the caves and crevices. Point out the smoke-blackened ceilings and ask them to imagine what it would have been like to live here. Bandelier wrote a novel, *The Delight Makers*, vividly depicting daily life in the canyon.

Before long, the cliff dwellings trail returns to the main part of the canyon and, after crossing the small stream, the Rito de los Frijoles, joins the wide path leading upstream to Alcove House (Ceremonial Cave). This path, well-marked by signs, is pleasant and very easy hiking. Towering ponderosa pines provide shade, and the nearby stream and rich vegetation are cool and refreshing. As you walk, ask children to be alert for Abert's squirrels, also called "tassel-eared" squirrels, a handsome gray species with a luxurious tail and tufted ears. Chipmunks and golden-mantled ground squirrels also are common. In the evening, deer often appear in the meadows, showing a conspicuous disregard for humans.

Alcove House (Ceremonial Cave) is reached after 0.75 mile from the junction with the Ruins Trail. Immediately after returning to the east side of the stream, you'll see the cave in the cliff above you, 150 feet above the valley floor. Aside from stairs at the bottom, you'll reach the cave in much the same way as the Indians did, by climbing pole ladders. Most children, except those afraid of heights, will love clambering up the wooden rungs.

At the top is a shallow cave whose walls have several small niches—storerooms and pens for turkeys—and in whose center is a restored underground chamber. Pottery sherds indicate the cave was inhabited from 1250 to 1600.

Why did the Indians locate here? No one knows for sure. As you sit in the shallow cave, look out across the canyon. My children say living here would have been like living in a tree house—without the tree.

Beyond Alcove House (Ceremonial Cave) the trail continues paralleling the Rito de los Frijoles in the narrow canyon. The clear stream passes beneath numerous scenic overhangs. There's more solitude here, as most visitors go no farther than Alcove House (Ceremonial Cave). Unfortunately, the rich vegetation along the stream includes poison ivy and stinging nettle, but don't let these deter you; instead, teach your children to recognize and avoid them.

To return to the visitor center, simply go back along the main trail. Overnight camping is not available in the canyon, but there is a campground on the mesa just above, and a steep but interesting and very scenic trail leads from the campground into the canyon.

19. Rito de los Frijoles Waterfalls

Type: Dayhike
Difficulty: Easy to moderate for children
Hikable: Year-round
One way: 2 miles
Starting elevation: 6,066 feet
High point: 6,121 feet
Map: Frijoles 7.5-minute USGS quad
Hazards: None

Most visitors to Bandelier National Monument come to see the cliff dwellings, described in hike 18. But there's more to the monument than ancient ruins: there's also this short hike to two waterfalls that rank among the most scenic in New Mexico. And along the way are some pleasant places to picnic and allow children to wade in the stream.

Like hike 18, this one begins at the Bandelier National Monument Visitor Center, reached by driving 3.3 miles from the monument's entrance over a very scenic road, with several overlooks into Cañon de los Frijoles. At the visitor center, cross the small stream, the Rito de los Frijoles, then turn left and walk through parking and picnic areas downhill, paralleling the stream, to where signs mark the

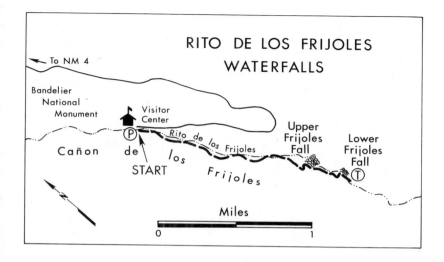

RITO DE LOS FRIJOLES
WATERFALLS

To NM 4

Bandelier
National
Monument

Visitor
Center

P

Cañon   de   los

START

Rito de los Frijoles

Frijoles

Upper
Frijoles
Fall

Lower
Frijoles
Fall

T

Miles

0   1

trailhead. The trail stays in the canyon, whose walls prohibit any chance of going astray.

The trail goes gently along the canyon's western lower slope, but soon it dips into the canyon bottom to follow the stream, crossing it several times. The rito, Spanish for "creek," even in the spring is a rather modest little stream as it burbles along through the narrow valley made green by its moisture. The Indians grew crops in tiny fields here, including the beans (*frijoles*) for which the canyon and the stream were named. Now hikers and picnickers seek shade beneath the ponderosas, sit beside the stream, and cool their feet.

But the tranquil, verdant valley and pleasant little stream end at Upper Frijoles Falls. Here the stream plunges over a basalt ledge, its water exploding into a waterfall larger than one would expect from the valley above. In less than 0.5 mile the stream plunges again over Lower Frijoles Falls. By now the ponderosas are gone, and the trail and the stream descend through a jagged, rocky gorge on their way to the Rio Grande below. The tortured rocks are a reminder of the violent volcanism that created this landscape.

Of the two falls, Upper Frijoles Falls clearly is the more scenic. It's higher—70 feet tall—and from the overlook it's beautifully framed as it passes between the walls of the canyon it has created. The black basalt, sometimes mottled with green, contrasts with buff volcanic tuff, dotted with holes formed by gas bubbles, and with yellow and ochre sedimentary layers.

Because of danger of falling rock, hikers are not allowed to go to the pool at the upper falls' base, but the view from the overlook along the trail invites lingering, despite being somewhat exposed to the sun.

Lower Frijoles Falls

If you were to continue down the trail, you would meet the Rio Grande after 0.75 mile, but the hike is steep, and in most seasons hot and exposed. Most parties with children will prefer to return and perhaps find a flat rock near the stream, letting the children dangle their feet in the stream's cool waters, the adults wondering how often in prehistoric times the same scene occurred in precisely the same spot.

20. Las Conchas Trail

Type: Dayhike
Difficulty: Easy for children
Hikable: April through October
One way: 2 miles
Starting elevation: 8,410 feet
Ending elevation: 8,400 feet
Maps: Santa Fe National Forest;
Redondo Peak 7.5-minute
USGS quad
Hazards: None

This is quintessential Jemez country: a mountain stream meandering through a lushly forested canyon whose flanks were created during an ancient volcanic eruption. It's easy hiking, with enough variety to hold everyone's interest.

This stretch of the Jemez River's East Fork can be approached via east and west routes, both trails heading on NM 4 about 5 miles apart and both culminating at the East Fork Box. The west route is described under hike 21; the Las Conchas route avoids wading the stream because the Santa Fe National Forest has built bridges over the crossings.

The Las Conchas (Spanish for "the shells") trailhead is on NM 4 about 11 miles east of its junction with NM 126 at La Cueva and about 15 miles west of its junction with NM 501 south of Los Alamos. The trailhead is on the north side of the road, just about 0.5 mile west of the Las Conchas Campground. Several other national forest campgrounds are located nearby along NM 4.

The trail starts on the stream's west side and is marked by a sign reading: "Las Conchas Trailhead, East Fork Box 2." A small sign nearby indicates this is Trail 137. Soon after a small wooden span over a

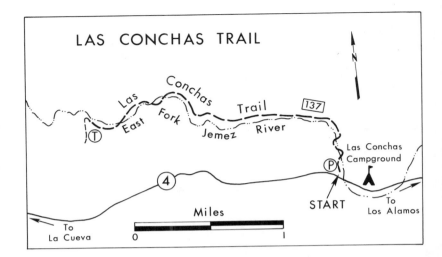

damp area, the trail encounters the first of six single-log bridges crossing the stream, clustered in threes toward the beginning and end of the hike. Children will look forward to walking across these.

The trail continues to follow the stream down the canyon, passing through broad meadows and beneath vertical rock formations. Point out to children that these were formed by ash from huge volcanic eruptions. About 5 million years ago, cataclysmic eruptions rocked

A log bridge over the East Fork of the Jemez River on the Las Conchas Trail

this region, covering the uplands with incandescent ash 1,000 feet thick over 400 square miles. As you walk through the cool, green valley today it's hard to imagine it as a lifeless, gray wasteland of steaming volcanic debris.

At 2 miles you encounter two signs, one pointing back toward the Las Conchas trailhead from which you've come, the other pointing uphill and indicating that the East Fork trailhead of Trail 137, which you've been following, is 3 miles away; this portion of the trail is steep initially but then becomes more gentle as it winds through the ponderosa forest. But most hikers, especially those with children, will go no farther than here, as just downstream and past a fence with a pass-through is the beginning of the gorge that is the East Fork Box.

Access to the box is difficult from here. A faint, unmarked trail climbs over the rocks on the stream's south side and then traverses along the upper hillside paralleling the box, but this trail is steep and rough. However, the head of the box is a beautiful place to linger. If the water's low, children can wade here—the stream enters the gorge by rippling over a tiny waterfall—and the meadow is filled with wildflowers. This stream also is inviting for fishing, though it's fished heavily. Return as you came; the hike back will go quickly.

21. East Fork Box

Type: Dayhike
Difficulty: Easy for children
Hikable: June through October
One way: 1.5 miles
Starting elevation: 7,947 feet
High point: 8,200 feet
Maps: Santa Fe National Forest; Redondo Peak 7.5-minute USGS quad
Hazards: Seasonally high water

This is a hike for old sneakers. The East Fork of the Jemez River here is a scenic little stream meandering through open ponderosa forest and grassy meadows and between volcanic cliffs. And while you can scramble behind the cliffs—the unmarked trails are faint and rough—it's much easier and a lot more fun simply to don old sneakers and wade the stream. This is possible, however, only after the spring runoff has subsided; by midsummer shallow fords can be crossed even by small children.

The East Fork trailhead is on NM 4 about 23 miles west of Los Alamos, 6 miles east of the intersection with NM 126 at La Cueva. A parking lot is on the highway's east side, where a Santa Fe National Forest sign indicates the East Fork of the Jemez River. This stream is a favorite with fishermen, as it's beautiful, accessible, and easy to fish, but for these reasons it's heavily fished.

The trail begins on the river's north side, but within 0.25 mile it makes the first of many crossings. At 0.75 mile the trail, back on the stream's north side, encounters a fence and a "Private Property-No Trespassing" sign. As the trail indicates, most hikers ignore this, but to accommodate the landowners the national forest has built a wooden bridge leading to an alternate trail that rejoins the stream 0.4 mile later (going along the stream is 0.25 mile). Unfortunately, this alternate trail is very steep, especially on the descent. Except for this detour, the hiking is level and easy, the trail paralleling the stream, flanked by grassy meadows interspersed with towering ponderosa pines.

At 1 mile from the highway along the stream is another wooden bridge, and just 100 yards farther is the entrance to the East Fork Box. Here the canyon walls become even more constricted but also more dramatic. The wading remains easy, however, until a series of deep pools is reached. In recent years, this site has become extremely popular, especially with young people seeking the excitement of leaping from the cliffs into the pools, and on summer weekends this area

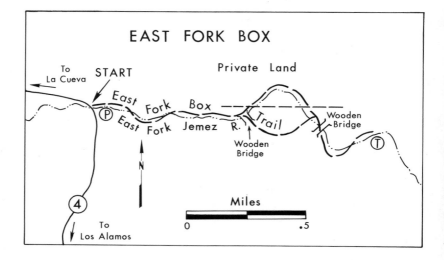

Hikers returning from the East Fork Box cross the East Fork of the Jemez River.

can be oppressively crowded. Beyond the pools some scrambling over the cliffs is required, but the cascade in the glade beyond is worth it. To go beyond this in the box, however, requires even more climbing to surmount the enclosing cliffs, with access to the river very limited, and most hikers go no farther.

So relax and let children play in the water here (you, too)—sliding over rocks, jumping in pools (not necessarily from the cliffs!), and wading in the stream. When they're back at the car, bundle them in warm, dry clothes, give them a big hug, and tell them about your own favorite wading experiences.

Note: Several national forest campgrounds are in the area: The nearest are the Jemez Falls Campground, less than 1 mile west on NM 4; the Redondo Campground a few miles farther west on NM 4; and, a few miles to the east on NM 4, the Las Conchas Campground.

22. McCauley Hot Spring

Type: Dayhike
Difficulty: Moderate for children
Hikable: May through October
One way: 2 miles
Starting elevation: 6,760 feet (Battleship Rock);
7,890 feet (Jemez Falls)
High point: 7,315 feet (for Battleship Rock route)
Maps: Santa Fe National Forest;
Jemez Springs and Redondo
Peak 7.5-minute USGS quads
Hazards: Infrequent poison ivy

This is my family's favorite New Mexico hot spring. The relatively easy hike is long enough to reduce overcrowding, the site is beautiful, the lukewarm water, estimated at 85 to 90 degrees Fahrenheit, is a perfect temperature for summer and fall, and the main pool is large enough for children to play in yet small and shallow enough even for toddlers.

McCauley Hot Spring, also known as Battleship Rock Hot Spring, sits on a high shelf of the Jemez Mountains and can be reached either by hiking up from Battleship Rock or by hiking down from Jemez Falls. Both start at Santa Fe National Forest picnic areas—there's camping at Jemez Falls—and both hikes are just under 2 miles. For dayhikes, I prefer to hike up to the hot spring, spend some time soaking, then finish the excursion with an easy downhill hike. If you choose the Jemez Falls trail, be sure to take the 0.5-mile hike to an overlook above Jemez Falls, one of the largest in New Mexico; it's an easy hike through ponderosa pines. Be sure to keep children away from the cliff's edge at the overlook.

Battleship Rock is reached by taking NM 4 for 6 miles northeast of Jemez Springs (the Jemez Falls turnoff is on NM 4 at 6 miles east of its junction with NM 126). Park at the Battleship Rock Picnic Area, cross the bridge, then walk beneath the prow of the ship-shaped cliff and past a gazebolike shelter to Trail 137, marked by a sign. This follows the left bank of the East Fork of the Jemez River, and in the spring portions can be underwater, requiring a detour. Also, several small, unmarked trails are near the river and Battleship Rock, so attempt to stay on the main trail. But after about 0.25 mile, Trail 137 leaves the river to switchback up the mountainside and is easy to follow.

The trail from the Jemez Falls campground is found just downslope from the toilet in the parking area.

As you hike the Battleship Rock trail, have children notice numerous volcanic boulders along the trail that look like huge chunks of crudely polished black glass; in fact, that's what they are. About 5 million years ago enormous volcanic eruptions created the Jemez Mountains, and occasionally the volcanic material was fused into volcanic glass, known as obsidian. Let children stroke the rock and feel its glassy smoothness. The tall pine trees around you are ponderosas; have children sniff the orange bark for its faint vanilla scent.

After about 1 mile the Battleship Rock trail winds over a relatively level shelf before climbing again to the final shelf where the spring is located. Just before the spring, look to your right at the piles of rounded stones, all that remain of ancient buildings that once housed the Pueblo Indians, who also visited the spring.

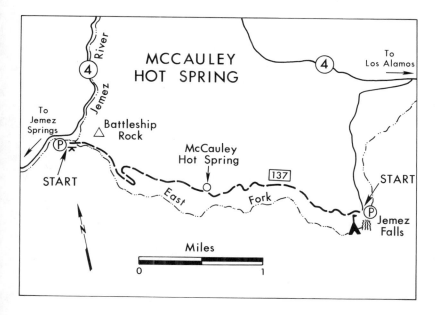

Almost immediately upon entering the lukewarm water children will notice tiny fish—guppies brought here by hikers. The main pool is fed by a spring issuing from the mountainside; downslope from this pool are several smaller but more private pools. As at most backcountry hot springs, swimsuits are optional; if you or your children are bothered by adult nudity you might choose one of these smaller pools or plan to visit the spring on a weekday, when the chances of privacy—and modesty—are much higher than on weekends. As at most moist locations in New Mexico, you should watch for infrequent poison ivy.

But these caveats notwithstanding, McCauley Hot Spring is among New Mexico's best, an enduring gift of the ancient volcanoes that created the Jemez Mountains.

23. Battleship Rock Waterfall

Type: Dayhike
Difficulty: Easy for children
Hikable: April through November
One way: 0.5 mile
Starting elevation: 6,760 feet
High point: 7,000 feet
Maps: Santa Fe National Forest; Jemez Springs 7.5-minute USGS quad
Hazards: Poison ivy

This very short hike combines well with other features in the area; there's a nice picnic area, Battleship Rock is scenic and interesting, and this is one of the trailheads for McCauley Hot Spring, hike 22. And for small children, the waterfall is a delightful little adventure.

To reach the Battleship Rock Picnic Area from the west, drive on NM 4 about 6 miles north from the village of Jemez Springs; from the east, drive 27.8 miles on NM 4 from the junction of NM 4 and NM 501. At the Battleship Rock Picnic Area, drive or walk across the bridge spanning the Jemez River and turn left immediately to the parking lot. At the far end of this a small brook joins the Jemez River. No signs or trail markers point to the waterfall, and indeed there's not one trail but rather a confusion of routes, but don't worry; just stay near the brook, not the river, and you can't go wrong. The brook flows through a tiny valley, increasingly flanked by volcanic cliffs,

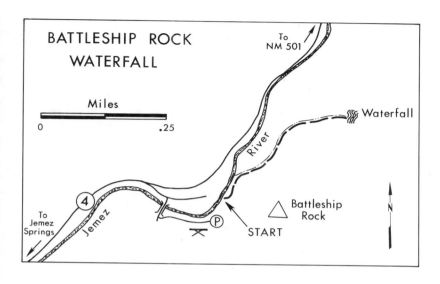

Poison ivy—don't touch!

beneath shady ponderosa pines and other trees. Poison ivy is among the plants taking advantage of the moisture here, but it's not abundant. The best protection against poison ivy is learning to recognize it; I've given my children a reward for every group of plants they spot.

The hiking sometimes is slippery, you'll cross the brook at least once, and after only 0.5 mile you'll come to the waterfall, a pleasant, child-sized cascade. On a hot day, the temptation to take an impromptu shower is almost irresistible, and it's a rare child who returns with dry feet from this hike.

24. San Pedro Parks

Type: Dayhike or backpack
Difficulty: Moderate to difficult for children
Hikable: June through October
One way: 5.5 miles
Starting elevation: 9,200 feet
High point: 10,040 feet
Maps: San Pedro Parks Wilderness (Santa Fe National Forest); Nacimiento Peak 7.5-minute USGS quad
Hazards: Summer thunderstorms

San Pedro Parks is a gentle wilderness. The terrain is rolling rather than rugged; the streams are child-sized; and the wildflower-filled meadows are aptly named parks.

The wilderness is reached from NM 44 at Cuba by taking NM 126 about 6.5 miles east to where the pavement ends. Follow this road, now dirt, another 1.5 miles to where Forest Road 70 goes north and after 4 miles arrives at Nacimiento Campground.

From the campground, the Vacas Trail 51 heads north and after slightly less than a mile of gentle ascent through spruce-fir forest comes to San Gregorio Reservoir, very popular with local fishermen.

The forest here is rich with fungi, and children will enjoy spotting different mushroom species. The deadly but colorful amanitas are common here; look for their orange-red caps covered with white flecks. But take a moment and discuss with your children the importance of never eating any wild mushroom. Despite the folklore they may

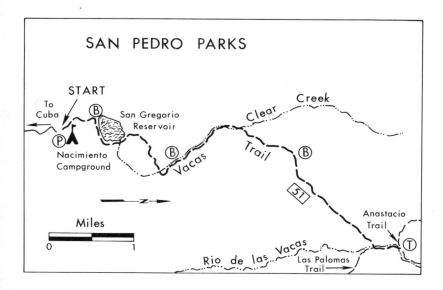

SAN PEDRO PARKS

START

To
Cuba

Ⓑ San Gregorio
Reservoir

Ⓟ

Nacimiento
Campground

Creek

Clear

Vacas

Trail

Ⓑ

51

Anastacio
Trail

Ⓣ

Miles

0   1

N→

Rio de las Vacas

Las Palomas
Trail →

hear—mushrooms are OK, toad-
stools are not; poisonous mushrooms will cause silver to darken;
the skin can be peeled easily from
the caps of non-poisonous mushrooms—the fact is there are no
reliable field rules for distinguish-
ing safe fungi from dangerous
ones. And amanitas are indeed
dangerous. One case has been
recorded in which a child died
from eating just one-third of the
top of an amanita.

The Vacas Trail continues
going north around the east side
of the lake, then bends east to join
Clear Creek. It parallels the
stream, soon entering an area of
aspen groves and meadows. This
is a natural place to break, turn
around, or camp.

After almost 2 miles from the
lake the Vacas Trail leaves Clear
Creek to pass through more forest, aspen groves, and meadows

A poisonous amanita *mushroom*
(Photo: Joel Pearson)

to arrive after 4.3 miles from the lake at the Rio de las Vacas (Spanish for "river of the cows") and the intersection with Las Palomas Trail 50. Just 0.2 mile farther is the terminus of Anastacio Trail 345.

Here again are the high meadows for which the San Pedro Parks Wilderness is known; these junctions are natural places to turn around or camp. This patchwork of meadows and forests is excellent habitat for wildlife, especially elk and deer, and if you're lucky you might see some. Have children look for their tracks and droppings along the trail and in mud near streams. I once found a bear track here. Water is abundant in the numerous streams meandering through the parks, but cattle graze throughout, and all drinking water must be treated thoroughly; better still, plan to bring water with you.

Also, though the terrain is gentle here, the weather often is not, especially in late summer during the "monsoon season," when thundershowers can occur every afternoon. But barring bad weather, the San Pedro Parks Wilderness is welcoming and friendly, a good place for easy hiking, for fishing in the lake and streams, for simply enjoying wild nature.

25. Kasha-Katuwe Tent Rocks National Monument

Type: Dayhike
Difficulty: Easy for children
Hikable: Year-round, best May, June, September, and October
One way: 1 mile
Starting elevation: 5,760 feet
High point: 7,100 feet
Maps: Santa Fe National Forest; Santo Domingo Pueblo and Cañada 7.5-minute USGS quads
Hazards: Flash floods during thundershowers

If a child were to redesign the Grand Canyon, it would look like Tent Rocks.

Bizarre, buff-colored rock formations look as if they were sculpted from soft-serve ice cream, while clefts only one person wide lead to hidden grottoes. In the soft volcanic tuff people have scratched mysterious symbols, while in the sand underfoot are pea-sized obsidian pebbles called "Apache tears."

The name itself—Tent Rocks—describes the weathered rock formations that resemble a tepee encampment. Tent rock formations are common throughout the Pajarito Plateau, but this is the most scenic concentration. Tent rocks were formed when large rocks sheltered the soft volcanic tuff beneath from erosion. Point out to children that many of the "tents" have a rock perched on top.

Tent Rocks is reached by driving Interstate 25 between Albuquerque and Santa Fe to the Cochiti Pueblo exit, then following signs to Cochiti Lake. Just beneath the Cochiti Lake dam, turn southwest on NM 22 and drive 1.5 miles to Cochiti Pueblo; as you approach the pueblo, tell children to look for water towers painted to resemble drums, conspicuous landmarks. Cochiti is the northernmost of the pueblos speaking the Keresan language; its members explain its name thus: "*Kotyete*, which means 'stone kiva,' is our native name. From our oral history we know that our ancestors inhabited Frijoles Canyon [in Bandelier National Monument] a few centuries before the Spanish visited us at our present location."

From the pueblo, Tribal Road 92 heads northwest to become Forest Road 266. At 5 miles, you will find the monument entrance on your right. By the entrance are parking, toilets, picnic tables, and information. Hike about 0.5 mile east into a small, enclosed valley, graced with ponderosa pines and ringed with cliffs and more tent rocks. Two canyons begin here. Their entrances are not obvious, so simply follow the sandy washes. Both canyons are fun to explore, but most people take the easternmost one. Encourage your children to explore the

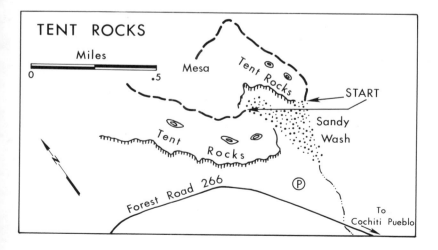

canyon gently; the volcanic tuff, which is compressed volcanic ash, is very soft and easily damaged. Vandals have even gouged graffiti into the stone. Have your children examine the tuff to see the volcanic fragments embedded in it.

In the gravel floor of the canyon are the Apache tears—small, rounded fragments of obsidian, a form of volcanic glass, that like the tuff was ejected from the cataclysmic eruptions that created the Pajarito Plateau. The Apache tears make great souvenirs of the hike for children.

This tiny, twisting canyon runs less than a mile, but like a stroll through an amusement park it seems much longer. Eventually, the narrow canyon opens up as it ascends to an arid, scrub-covered mesa. The fantasy's over, until you descend.

Tent Rocks covers almost 12,000 acres, most owned by the U.S. Bureau of Land Management, which has designated the site a special management area. Only day use is permitted, and there are no facilities such as toilets or water.

Albuquerque Area

The prickly pear cactus in bloom

26. Domingo Baca Canyon

Type:	Dayhike or backpack
Difficulty:	Moderate for children
Hikable:	Year-round, best in cooler months
One way:	2 miles
Starting elevation:	6,200 feet
High point:	7,500 feet
Maps:	Sandia Mountain Wilderness (Cibola National Forest); Sandia Crest 7.5-minute USGS quad
Hazards:	Poison ivy

Whenever I hike this foothills trail with my children, I always point out the bear grass—kid-sized clumps of graceful, sinuous leaves. Bears like to dig the tuberous roots of this plant, hence the name. The likelihood of seeing bears is slight but not impossible, even on a trail so close to Albuquerque, and the bear grass is a reminder that the city has a true wilderness area in its backyard, and from the little canyon to which this trail leads, the city seems distant indeed.

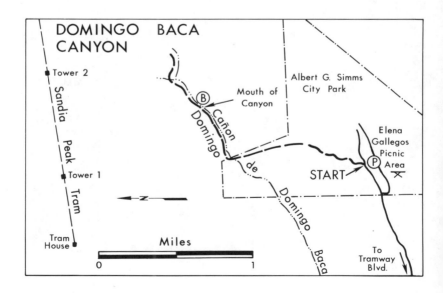

In northeast Albuquerque, drive north on Tramway Boulevard past Montgomery Boulevard for 1.8 miles to the paved road branching right and leading to the Elena Gallegos Picnic Area and the Albert G. Simms City Park. These are operated by the Albuquerque Parks and Recreation Department, which charges a $1 fee per vehicle, $2 on weekends; an annual pass is available. The Domingo Baca Trail heads northeast from the parking area and is well marked by signposts.

As you drive here, your children might ask about the names. No one knows who Domingo Baca was, perhaps a shepherd who grazed his flocks here, but Elena Gallegos was an important woman in local history. She was a member of a family that returned to New Mexico in 1692 with the Reconquest after the Pueblo Revolt. Later, a widow, she acquired 70,000 acres of a Spanish land grant. Subsequently, the lands became known as the Elena Gallegos Grant. Elena Gallegos died in 1731. Eventually, much of the land was acquired by Albuquerque Academy. In the 1980s, with this valuable open space threatened by development, Albuquerque voters approved a quarter-cent sales tax to purchase the land. It now is administered by the U.S. Forest Service and the City of Albuquerque.

From the picnic area, the trail crosses a gravelly wash, usually dry, and briefly joins a dirt road. The trail leaves the road at a T to continue northeast, where it takes a rolling course over open piñon-juniper foothills, past granite monoliths, toward the jagged cliffs of the west face of the Sandias. Domingo Baca Canyon, your destination, is easy to spot; it's the canyon beneath the Sandia Peak Tram towers. As children hike they can watch for the tram cars that seem to float up and down the mountain's face. On most good-weather days, colorful hang gliders gyre on the upsweeping warm air currents. At 1.25 miles you reach a tiny stream. You could follow it into the canyon, but it's easier to stay on the trail for another 0.25 mile north before following the trail east 0.5 mile to the canyon's mouth.

Here the canyon narrows abruptly. My family usually stops at the canyon's mouth to let the children explore the stream and climb the smooth granite boulders, while the adults enjoy the refreshing canyon coolness as well as the views of the Sandia cliffs. Moisture-loving poison ivy grows near the stream but is not abundant. At the canyon's mouth are the stone foundations of an old cabin—perhaps once used by Domingo Baca!

At 0.25 mile into the canyon the trail briefly leaves the stream, branching right and going up a short, steep bank. This junction is not marked and is difficult to find, but it's worth searching for, as the trail soon becomes distinct again, and the little forested stream it leads to after 0.25 mile is delightful. This stream flows through a narrow canyon that runs almost a mile back toward the cliffs; it's lined with lush, green vegetation and has several tiny waterfalls. Yet someone viewing the Sandias from the west would not suspect the canyon existed, deceived by distance and relief into believing the Sandias' west face to be just a barren wall. The western Sandias have many such canyon surprises, and upper Domingo Baca Canyon is among the best. It's fun for children to explore, and the gnarled oaks are great for climbing. Here also are several good camping sites. Though this is primarily a dayhike, it also makes an easy, low-risk overnighter—and your car will be safe in the patrolled parking lot.

I cannot count the times my family has been to Domingo Baca Canyon, yet it remains a favorite. Perhaps that's because it always seems to have something new to offer. That, and perhaps because of the wonder that it exists, wild and beautiful, so near to Albuquerque.

27. Embudo Canyon

Type: Dayhike
Difficulty: Easy to moderate for children
Hikable: Year-round
One way: 3 miles
Starting elevation: 6,200 feet
High point: 7,600 feet
Maps: Sandia Mountain Wilderness (Cibola National Forest); Tijeras 7.5-minute USGS quad
Hazards: None

Probably the Sandia Mountains hike most easily accessible from Albuquerque, and for that reason among the most popular, Embudo Canyon features easy walking, a tiny but pleasant stream, dramatic views, and rocks that children love to scramble on.

The trailhead for Embudo Trail 193 is reached by taking Indian School Boulevard east from Tramway Boulevard until it ends at the large parking lot. A plethora of unmarked trails diverge here, but most converge back in the canyon; indeed, the Spanish *embudo* means "funnel."

At a large sign marking Albuquerque Open Space, begin hiking east over a former roadbed toward the large, obvious water storage tank. Just to the south of this is a water catchment dam; my children always love to scramble up the long concrete slope.

After 0.5 mile from the trailhead you pass a fence and a sign

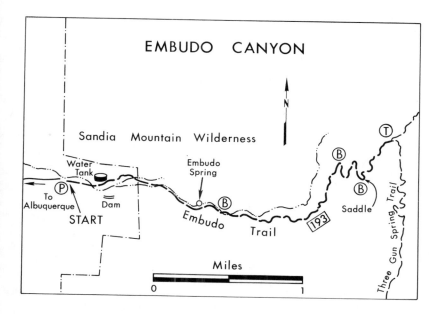

marking the Sandia Mountain Wilderness boundary. The route just past the wilderness boundary is a broad wash paved with the gravel derived from the decomposed granite of the Sandias. Similar washes enter the main wash from tributary canyons. Though usually dry, these washes are reminders of the flash floods that periodically issue from the narrow canyons above.

Have children look at the dusty green plants abundant along the trail. In late summer and fall they will be covered with tiny yellow flowers. These plants are the chamisas so well known in New Mexico. Their English name is rabbitbrush. If your children look closely at the flowers, they'll see the flowers have no petals but rather are clusters of what are known as "disk flowers," giving the flowers the appearance of fuzzy yellow woolly worms. The flowers have a heavy scent that many people dislike but that attracts insects. Navajo Indians make a yellow dye from the blossoms.

Another plant for children to notice along this hike is the cactus known as cholla (CHOY-yah). You can't miss cholla; they are tall and many-branched, the thorns sticking out all along the branches. In the spring they have beautiful, large magenta flowers, followed later by yellow convoluted fruits. When cholla die, they leave behind skeletons of their branches, perforated by scores of tiny holes. Children might like to take some home as souvenirs.

As you hike up the wash, the broad canyon narrows like the mouth of a funnel. The water here has carved a deep gouge in the gravel, creating a mini-canyon, and sometimes children like to play in this, jumping into the soft earth, but don't let them tunnel into it as the gravel is very unstable and can collapse.

After about 0.4 mile from the wilderness boundary you come to Embudo Spring, where water trickles from a masonry wall. Here the canyon is constricted between huge, steep granite boulders. Rock climbers often practice here, and children will like to watch them. The hiking route can be confusing here but stays near the canyon's bottom, and the constriction lasts only 0.25 mile before the canyon opens up again. Many parties either stop here or, at the top of the constriction, take a brief diversion by walking up the sandy arroyo. Many cacti and desert plants bloom here in the summer.

Above the constriction, Trail 193 crosses the sandy streambed to follow a relatively gentle rolling course along the canyon's south side for about 1 mile, entering a broad and scenic basin from which Albuquerque, less than 2 miles away, is not visible. You're in a wilderness area, after all. Toward the back of the basin the trail suddenly ascends steeply. Most hikers will have no problems here, but short stretches are very steep and rocky. You might want to break here before continuing. After 0.5 mile you'll reach the ridge or saddle separating Embudo and Three Gun Spring canyons. The views here are spectacular, and this is a natural place to break.

At the ridge, the trail switchbacks northeast and up, always climbing, sometimes steeply, until after about 0.4 mile it reaches the

Claret cup cactus

intersection with the Three Gun Spring Trail. The best views, how-ever, are at the ridge, and tired hikers will find little beyond to justify the extra 1-mile round-trip.

28. North Sandia Peak

Type: Dayhike
Difficulty: Easy to moderate for children
Hikable: May through October
One way: 2 miles
Starting elevation: 10,678 feet
Ending elevation: 10,447 feet
Maps: Sandia Mountain Wilderness (Cibola National Forest); Sandia Crest 7.5-minute USGS quad
Hazards: Cliffs

This hike in many ways resembles hike 29 to the Sandia Peak Tram: both are along the Crest Trail 130; both begin at the Crest House; both are about the same distance; and both feature spectacular views of the Sandia escarpment and the Rio Grande Valley. The main difference is that this hike, lacking the tram, attracts far fewer people, though it still is among the most popular trails in the Sandias.

The Sandia Crest is reached by driving east from Albuquerque on Interstate 40, taking the Tijeras exit to NM 14, driving north for 6 miles to NM 536, then following signs for 12 miles to the crest parking lot. Cibola National Forest–Sandia Ranger District charges a $3 parking fee at all trailheads.

From here, walk north toward the radio tower complex, but instead of entering it go down the pavement about 50 feet to a sign that indicates Trail 130.

The trail is level at the beginning, passing through a wildflower-filled meadow, but soon it enters the forest and goes gently downhill. The main trail is easy to follow through the woods, though numerous smaller, unmarked trails digress briefly to the west to overlooks from the crest. These overlooks are good for breaks, but parents should keep smaller children from the edges. At some seasons, ladybugs swarm on shrubs along here, and children will love seeing a bush orange with thousands of ladybugs.

At 1.25 miles, as the main trail again begins descending into the forest, a faint branch trail leads uphill to the northwest, coming out

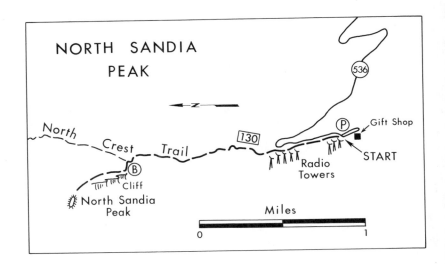

after a few hundred yards atop a cliff whose level, open top runs north. Most parties will want to go no farther. The views from here are spectacular, especially of the huge rock face called the Shield. Point out to children the white limestone layer capping the Sandias here; the cliffs on which they're standing once were at the bottom of the ocean, and the limestone contains fossil seashells. But keep children away from the edge, as the drop-off is precipitous.

North Sandia Peak, at 10,447 feet, is farther north and slightly west, though the route isn't well marked. The summit is mostly forested, but if you hike west just about 25 feet down some rock ledges you come to an overlook offering spectacular views into Del Agua Canyon and the west face of the northern Sandias. But again, keep children away from the edges.

Child-size shelter on the Crest Trail

From this vantage point, looking at the limestone ledges and the granite cliffs beneath, you might talk to children about the name Sandia. In Spanish it means "watermelon," but exactly why these mountains have that name is something of a mystery. One explanation attributes this name to watermelons or watermelon-resembling gourds growing in canyons here. Another suggests it was transferred from El Corazon de la Sandia, a mountain in the Spanish Sierra Nevada resembling the heart of a watermelon. An explanation believed by the Sandia Pueblo Indians is that the Spaniards, when they encountered the pueblo in 1540, called it Sandia because they thought the squash growing there were watermelons. But the most widely accepted explanation is that the Sandia Mountains, especially when viewed from the northwest at evening, resemble a sliced watermelon, the granite pink with alpenglow, capped by a white limestone layer and covered with dark green vegetation resembling a rind. Ask children if they can see a resemblance to a watermelon slice in the mountains.

Returning the same way you came is mostly uphill, but at the hike's end is the Sandia Crest, with a snack bar, gift shop, observation point, hang glider launching site, and much more to make a child's hiking adventure complete.

---

29. Crest House to Sandia Peak Tram

Type: Dayhike
Difficulty: Easy for children
Hikable: May through October
One way: 1.5 miles
Starting elevation: 10,678 feet
Ending elevation: 10,300 feet
Maps: Sandia Mountain Wilderness (Cibola National Forest); Sandia Crest 7.5-minute USGS quad
Hazards: Cliffs

The Sandia Crest often has a carnival atmosphere: hang glider pilots leaping from cliffs, backpackers, mountain runners, tourists from everywhere snapping photos and sightseeing.

Indeed, during the summer it often seems most residents of Albuquerque have sought respite here, at 10,678 feet, from the in-

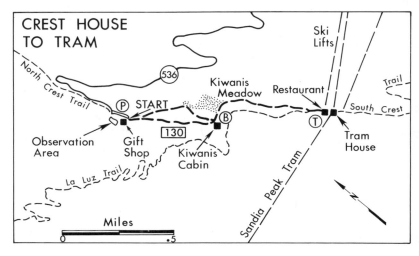

tense heat below. But for all the crowds and commotion, this trail never fails to delight—especially children.

The Sandia Crest is reached by driving east from Albuquerque on Interstate 40, taking the Tijeras exit to NM 14, driving north for 6 miles to NM 536, then following signs for 12 miles to the crest parking lot. Cibola National Forest–Sandia Ranger District charges a $3 parking fee at all trailheads.

Here are rest rooms, an interesting gift shop with refreshments, and an observation area for the Sandia escarpment and the Rio Grande Valley below. Just north of the parking area is where hang gliders often begin their flights, taking advantage of the thermals sweeping up the west face of the mountains, and children will love watching the hang glider pilots launch themselves into space from the cliffs.

Several trails meet at Sandia Crest: the west-face La Luz Trail, the North Crest Trail, which is hike 28 in this book, and this route connecting the Crest House with the Sandia Peak Tram. It begins just south of the gift shop parking lot, and Crest Trail 130 is well marked. Two routes are offered: one through the forest and the other atop the crest's cliffs. The cliff trail, more scenic and interesting, is not really dangerous if toddlers are kept back from the edge—and the views are truly breathtaking. Also, observation points with guardrails are along the route. Have children notice the vegetation atop the cliffs, and ask them if they can explain why the cliff tops are bare, while just a few yards away is forest. The answer is that the prevailing winds are from the west, and on a gusty day it will be obvious why the cliff plants keep a low profile.

Also mention to children the difference elevation makes in climate. Around them are trees and flowers that also are found in Alaska, yet below them in the valley are plants that also grow in Mexico—all because the mountain is a mile higher than the valley. If the Sandia Mountains were 3,000 feet higher, the plants would resemble those of the Arctic.

After 0.5 mile is the stone shelter called Kiwanis Cabin. Here or at Kiwanis Meadow just to the east is a good place to break or turn around. Gnarled trees make great climbing for children, and you can watch the Sandia Tram cars shuttling on their cables. In the limestone here children frequently can find fossils, usually the segmented stems of crinoids, a reminder that 300 million years ago this mountaintop was at the bottom of an ocean. From here they'll also be able to visualize the forces that created the Sandia Mountains. Ask them to imagine the fist of an underground giant pushing up the blocks in a sidewalk from beneath. As the blocks part and rise, the side facing the crack beneath the fist becomes rough and jagged while the rest of the blocks slope gradually away from the crack. Something like that created the Sandias, where a huge block rose on the west, leaving the block's top to slope gently away to the east.

The precipitous and rocky west face of the Sandias once was home to bighorn sheep. Persons riding the tram delighted in looking for the sure-footed animals, but disease eventually destroyed the herd, and no animals have been seen in recent years, though people continue to look for them. Deer, however, are common, and they often are seen in the meadow here.

Hikers ascending limestone ledges on the Crest Trail

From the meadow the trail enters pleasant forest. Look for signs pointing out ecological features. Regrettably, many trees and rocks along the trail bear the scars of humans seeking cheap immortality with a penknife.

At about 1.5 miles you reach the terminus of the Sandia Peak Tram (elevation 10,300 feet). The restaurant serves meals, snacks, and beverages, and there's an observation area. The Crest Trail continues south from here, but it's slightly steeper.

If you really want an adventure, don't drive to the Sandia Crest but take the tram from the bottom, do the hike in reverse, and then take the tram back down.

---

30. Tree Spring Trail

Type:	Dayhike
Difficulty:	Moderate for children
Hikable:	April through October
One way:	1.8 miles
Starting elevation:	8,480 feet
High point:	9,450 feet
Maps:	Sandia Mountain Wilderness (Cibola National Forest); Sandia Crest 7.5-minute USGS quad
Hazards:	Cliffs at lookout

To a child, reaching the dramatic Sandia Mountain crest and standing atop its cliffs will feel like a major mountaineering achievement, but the trail leading here is only 1.8 miles long, and nowhere is it difficult or steep. The Tree Spring Trail is by far the shortest, easiest hiking route to the Sandia Crest, a perfect introductory hike for children.

The trailhead is reached by driving east from Albuquerque on Interstate 40, exiting onto NM 14 at Tijeras, and driving 6 miles north to the intersection with NM 536 leading toward Sandia Crest. After driving 5.7 miles on NM 536 you reach the Tree Spring Trailhead on the left. Parking and toilets are available here. Cibola National Forest–Sandia Ranger District charges a $3 parking fee at all trailheads.You might be deceived by the name into looking for a spring here, but in fact the spring for which the trail was named is about 0.25 mile away.

The Tree Spring Trail 147 is well marked at the trailhead, and its lower section is easy, with a very modest gradient. After 0.25 mile

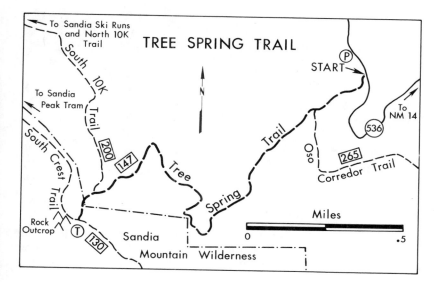

the Oso Corredor Trail 265, leading to the Faulty Trail 195, enters from the south, but you continue west. The trail ascends gradually through a forest of Douglas fir, ponderosa pine, aspen, and scrub oak.

Later, you'll encounter some steeper sections, nothing serious, but perhaps these are good times to play your favorite trail games with your children, or tell one of your favorite trail stories. At about 1.8 miles you reach the Sandia Mountain Wilderness boundary and the south terminus of the South 10K Trail 200. This easy trail leads through forest and the Sandia Ski Area ski runs to link up with the North 10K Trail at NM 536. It's called the 10K Trail because it stays around 10,000 feet for most of its distance.

And just beyond the 10K Trail junction the Tree Spring Trail intersects the Crest Trail 130. This leads south 13 miles to end at Canyon Estates; to the north it goes 1 steep mile to reach the Sandia Peak Tram. For strong hikers this can be an excellent round-trip, with a break in the middle at the tram's High Finance Restaurant.

But most people hiking the Tree Spring Trail are content to ignore these trails and just continue west 50 yards to a conspicuous rock outcropping overlooking the west escarpment of the Sandias.

From here are views of the Rio Grande Valley almost a mile below; closer are jagged granite cliffs, as well as the limestone layers capping them. Look in the limestone beneath your feet for the fossil remains of crinoid stems. Tell children these fossils are evidence that the rock on which they are sitting was once beneath an ocean. They might find it hard to imagine—I know I do—but it illustrates the vast scale of geologic changes over the immensity of time.

The west face of the Sandia Mountains from the overlook at the end of the Tree Spring Trail

On many good-weather days you'll see hang gliders riding the thermals created by westerly winds encountering the Sandias. You're just as likely to see ravens, hawks, and even golden eagles soaring on the ascending air.

Hiking back down the Tree Spring Trail will seem fast—even for children.

31. Travertine Waterfall—South Crest Trail

Type: Dayhike
Difficulty: Easy for children
Hikable: Year-round
One way: 0.5 mile
Starting elevation: 6,540 feet
High point: 6,840 feet
Maps: Sandia Mountain Wilderness (Cibola National Forest); Tijeras 7.5-minute USGS quad
Hazards: Poison ivy

Imagine yourself a toddler, and this half-mile hike will seem an expedition, the tiny cave at its end will seem a cavern, and the tiny trickling waterfall a water wonder.

To reach the South Crest Trail from Albuquerque, drive about 6

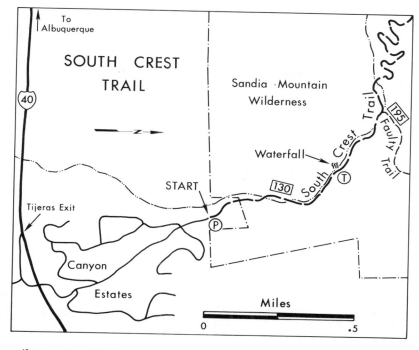

miles east on Interstate 40 and take the Tijeras exit, but instead of entering the village, turn left immediately, pass beneath the interstate overpass, bend right, and follow a good dirt road through the Canyon Estates residential development. After 0.5 mile, at the road's end, you reach the well-marked Cibola National Forest trailhead and parking area. Cibola National Forest–Sandia Ranger District charges a $3 parking fee at all trailheads.

This is the southern terminus of the 28-mile Crest Trail 130, but you'll be walking only 0.5 mile or slightly more, so find a leisurely pace and focus on the plants around you. There are piñons, oaks, ponderosas, wild grapes, asters, foxgloves, and many more.

There's also poison ivy in abundance, especially near the trail's moist sections. Don't despair over this but rather view it as an opportunity to educate yourself and certainly your children as to this common hazard. People often assume, mistakenly, that because poison ivy prefers moist habitats it is rare in an arid state such as New Mexico, but in fact it is almost ubiquitous along streams and moist canyons in the state. I have taught my children to recognize poison ivy by using a game. When we approach an area where I know poison ivy exists, I announce I will award them points—or treats—for each stand of poison ivy they locate. Their plant awareness advances rapidly.

The South Crest Trail ascends gradually from the parking area, crossing a small watercourse that's usually dry, and after about 0.5 mile arrives at a small cliff in the base of which are several grottoes and down which trickles a tiny waterfall. The cliff is made of travertine, a soft mineral formed by the evaporation of water containing dissolved limestone. Relax in the cool shade, and let the children explore.

Above the waterfall, the stream is pleasant and shaded, worth a visit, but be especially careful of poison ivy here. At the top of the waterfall, have children look in the light-colored sedimentary limestone for abundant fossils—crinoid stems and seashells.

Though the stream soon vanishes, the Crest Trail continues up the canyon, passing through a dry oak-piñon-juniper forest. After 0.25 mile, the Faulty Trail 195 branches right.

But for hikers with children, the main attractions are back along the brief, tiny stream, at the cave, waterfall, fossils, and, yes, even the poison ivy. Adults may view it as just a pleasant stroll, but a toddler will remember it as a bold, exciting adventure.

Travertine grottoes in the southeastern Sandia Mountains

32. Three Gun Spring

Type: Dayhike
Difficulty: Moderate for children
Hikable: Year-round, best April through June and September through November
One way: 1.75 miles
Starting elevation: 6,325 feet
High point: 7,400 feet
Maps: Sandia Mountain Wilderness (Cibola National Forest); Tijeras 7.5-minute USGS quad
Hazards: None

The name Three Gun Spring comes from someone long ago having carved the outline of three pistols into a wooden water trough here. The carvings are long gone, but the pleasant spring remains. Children enjoy collecting sprigs of wild mint here, and the hike is a delightful tour of the Upper Sonoran life zone.

To reach the Three Gun Spring trailhead, drive east on Interstate 40 from Albuquerque to the Carnuel exit, then take NM 333 east into Tijeras Canyon 2 miles to Montecello Estates, where you'll turn left

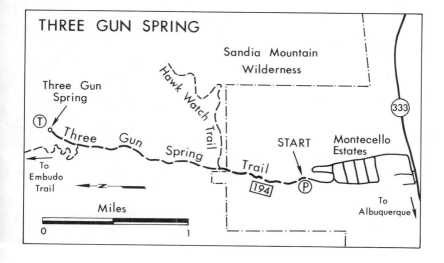

There are excellent climbing rocks on the way to Three Gun Spring.

and follow U.S. Forest Service signs to Three Gun Spring Trail 194. A road in a gravelly wash leads to a small parking area, with no parking fee. Regrettably, thieves have been known to target cars here, so don't leave your vehicle with your belongings visible—or take them with you.

You'll be hiking north, and soon after the parking area, the route branches left to leave the dry wash for a small ridge. Point out to children how the plants of the Upper Sonoran life zone—bear grass, gambel oak, junipers, and mountain mahogany—grow in clusters, the plants sheltering each other from the intense sun and desiccating air and cooperating to create cooler, moister microclimates. Jackrabbits and cottontails are abundant along this trail, especially in spring, and rare is the hike in which several are not seen. Prickly pear cacti also are common, with their oblong purple fruits in the fall. These fruits are edible and often delicious though filled with hard seeds, but like the rest of the cactus they're covered with tiny stickers that while not painful are an uncomfortable annoyance, especially stuck in a child's tongue. Wear gloves and peel the fruit with a knife before eating it.

Three Gun Spring Canyon is bounded on the east and west by ridges dotted with huge gray granite boulders that always have reminded me of immobilized elephants. Some of these boulders have tumbled into the canyon where they're perfect climbing rocks for children. But the same knobs and crystals that make for great handholds and toeholds also can scrape unprotected knees; have children wear long pants if they want to climb.

After 0.5 mile along the trail you'll come to a fence and a sign indicating the boundary of the Sandia Mountain Wilderness; the Hawk Watch Trail, hike 33, branches east from here. Continue north on the main trail another mile, crossing the sandy wash to another sign, this one indicating a side trail leading 0.25 mile into the narrow canyon to the spring. The main trail ascends a mile of switchbacks up the ridge to the junction with Embudo Trail 193; the views are spectacular from the junction, but the trail is steep. Parties with children likely will go no farther than the spring, shaded and moist. The spring often is little more than a seep or a trickle, but it nonetheless waters a wide variety of moisture-loving plants, including wild mint, willows, and cottonwoods. You'll be thirsty, but plan to drink water you brought with you, not the spring water.

When you return, consider forgoing the trail and instead following downhill one of several dry, sandy washes leading to the parking area. Children will love leaping and playing in the sand. And if you can acquire magnets, bring them, as children will enjoy running the magnets through the sand so that the abundant iron filings cling to them, like black woolly worms.

Three Gun Spring is pleasant in summer, but the canyon's southern exposure makes the trail very hot. The trail often is icy and muddy in winter, and the vegetation is somewhat drab then. So choose a morning or afternoon in the spring or fall and enjoy the southern Sandias.

33. Hawk Watch Trail

Type: Dayhike
Difficulty: Moderate to difficult for children
Hikable: Year-round, best during migration, February through May
One way: 2 miles
Starting elevation: 6,325 feet
High point: 7,500 feet
Maps: Sandia Mountain Wilderness (Cibola National Forest); Tijeras 7.5-minute USGS quad
Hazards: None

In all of western North America, only a few sites act as natural route funnels for migratory raptors—and this southern ridge of the Sandia Mountains is one of them. Here a combination of prevailing

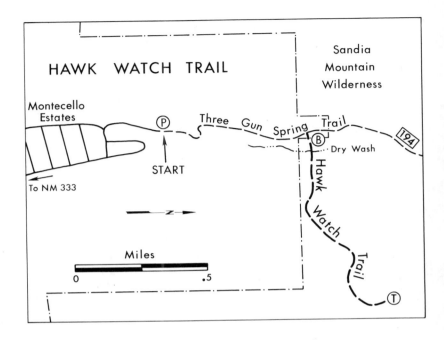

westerly winds and mountain topography causes raptor migration routes to converge. From late February through early May, literally thousands of hawks, kites, falcons, eagles, and other raptors, flying northward, soar over the knob reached by the appropriately named Hawk Watch Trail. Young children will find the trail difficult, the watching boring, but older children and adults can find excitement and wonder.

The trail is reached from the Three Gun Spring Trail, hike 32. Hike the Three Gun Spring Trail about 0.5 mile to the sign indicating the Sandia Wilderness boundary. At this sign the Hawk Watch Trail, marked by a sign, branches right to head downhill and east. The trail crosses a dry wash, then winds persistently up the canyon's east flank to arrive after about 1.5 miles at a level spot high on the mountain.

Even without the birds overhead, the Hawk Watch Trail makes an excellent hike in fall and winter, when the air is cool and clear. Before looking up for the birds, take time to acquaint children with the Upper Sonoran life zone of the southern Sandias. Watch for plants such as Apache plume, gambel oak, piñon, juniper, mountain mahogany, bear grass, yucca, and cholla. Roadrunners often are seen on this trail, and all children love to see these unusual birds striding over the ground; the Spanish name for these birds is *camino correr,* which means the same as the English name. Roadrunners do fly for short distances, but they're much more at home as pedestrians. Cottontail rabbits and jackrabbits also are common here. Ask children how the local rabbits must feel, with so many hawks and falcons flying overhead!

But beginning in late February most hikers will look mostly skyward, for then the raptors begin to arrive. Eagles are first, only a few in the beginning, then more each day until on peak days 40 eagles sometimes can be seen. Between 200 and 450 golden eagles, and seven or eight bald eagles, pass by during the spring migration.

Then come the hawks, falcons, and other raptors, as many as twenty species in all, including such rarities as the zone-tailed hawk and the black-shouldered kite.

The migration peaks during the first two weeks of April, when as many as 400 birds can be seen on a single day and as many as 4,000 birds can be tallied in one season. The birds can be fickle, however; on some days, especially stormy ones, few birds will be seen. Most of the birds fly along a ridge high above the watch site, and binoculars are needed to see them well. But the watchers often place a fake owl at the site, and raptors, which despise owls, sometimes come to investigate, flying just overhead.

Steve Hoffman of HawkWatch International with a raptor that was trapped and then banded at the Hawk Watch site

As the migration intensifies, HawkWatch International, a raptor conservation group, hires observers to be at the site 12 hours a day. The public is welcome to join them, and experienced bird-watchers usually are here to answer questions. But the Hawk Watch Trail, while not long, can be strenuous. Bring liquids and sun protection— and binoculars and field guides. And plan to spend some time. Watching for raptors is akin to fishing: patience is the key to success.

Raptors such as eagles, hawks, and falcons have an almost universal appeal—who would not thrill to seeing a bald eagle soaring?—but researchers with the raptor conservation group have a very serious purpose in trying to monitor the status of these birds. Explain to children that because raptors are at the top of the food chain, they are very sensitive to changes in the environment, such as contamination by pesticides. They're like natural barometers. When raptor populations decline, we know changes are occurring that threaten the entire ecosystem, including ourselves.

34. Rio Grande Nature Center

Type: Dayhike
Difficulty: Easy for children
Hikable: Year-round
Round-trip: 0.8-mile to 1-mile loops
Starting elevation: 4,965 feet
High point: 4,975 feet
Map: Los Griegos 7.5-minute USGS quad
Hazards: None

One of the best natural areas in New Mexico for seeing waterfowl and small wild animals is located, surprisingly, in the center of Albuquerque.

The Rio Grande bosque (pronounced BOSS-kay), Spanish for "forest," is a wilderness area 100 miles long and 0.5 mile wide that because of periodic flooding has been protected from development, even in the middle of the state's largest city. Once inside the bosque you'll discover the Rio Grande little changed from what the Spaniards encountered 450 years ago.

The best place to experience the bosque is at the Rio Grande

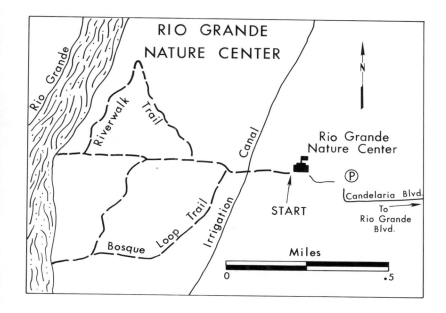

Nature Center, at the end of Candelaria Boulevard, west from Rio Grande Boulevard, north of Interstate 40.

The center charges a small fee (the trails are free) and offers interpretive exhibits, self-guiding trail booklets, an herb garden, and indoor and outdoor observation sites from which to watch waterfowl. My children have always delighted especially in the turtles sunning themselves on logs. The center also conducts hikes specifically for children on weekends.

The center maintains two trails, both starting at the center and leading through the bosque west to the Rio Grande. The Bosque Loop Trail is 0.8 mile long and is marked by blue numbers on the nature-trail stakes. The Riverwalk Trail is 1 mile long and has red numbers on the stakes. Both trails coincide until separating soon after a bridge that crosses an irrigation canal.

The sandy alluvial soil of the bosque is excellent for recording animal tracks, and the bosque is filled with other signs of animal life—woodpecker holes, beaver-gnawed trees, feathers, burrows. Children will love looking for them and will not be disappointed.

The most common trees of the bosque are cottonwoods, willows, Russian olive, and tamarisk. The last two are imports. Ask children to notice how they've adapted and thrived in this alien land. Tamarisk, also known as salt cedar, was imported into this country from Eurasia; it was first seen growing along the Pecos River in New Mexico in 1915. Since then it's spread along virtually all the state's major lower waterways and is regarded as a pest because it uses a great deal of water and crowds out native species. It's one of many examples of how the well-intentioned introduction of an exotic species can backfire.

Both trails end at the river. The Rio Grande is very shallow in parts, but near the shore it is usually deep and the current swift; keep children away from the edge. The Rio Grande is New Mexico's greatest river; its name in the languages of many of the state's Native Americans means the same as the Spanish name, "big river."

At the river children can see water birds such as herons, ducks, and Canada geese. It's a timeless scene, and you'll almost forget that a metropolitan area of half a million people is just a few hundred yards away. It's a powerful statement about the persistence and resilience of wild nature.

35. Piedras Marcadas Canyon— Petroglyph National Monument

Type: Dayhike
Difficulty: Easy for children
Hikable: Year-round
One way: 1.3 miles
Starting elevation: 5,200 feet
High point: 5,300 feet
Maps: Petroglyph National Monument; Los Griegos 7.5-minute USGS quad
Hazards: Sharp volcanic rocks

This hike is a delight for persons of all ages, for who could resist the adventure of searching for mysterious signs left by ancient people?

Petroglyphs are figures or designs scratched or pecked into rock. Beginning 4,000 years ago, Indians living along the Rio Grande started creating petroglyphs on the volcanic rocks of Albuquerque's West Mesa. Most petroglyphs were created during the period A.D. 1300–1700 by Pueblo Indians whose descendants still live along the Rio Grande, yet exactly why they were created remains a mystery, as does the meaning of many of the figures.

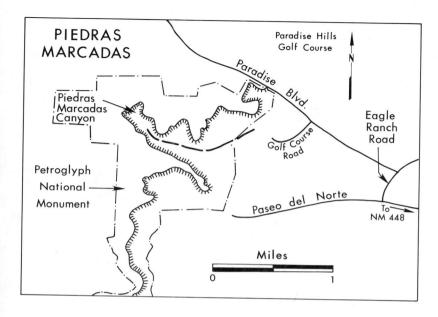

Whatever the reason, it was compelling, for 15,000 to 17,000 petroglyphs are found along the volcanic escarpment. To protect this extraordinary archaeological treasure against vandalism and development, Petroglyph National Monument was created in 1990.

Though petroglyphs are found throughout the monument, a high concentration is in Piedras Marcadas (Spanish for "marked rocks") Canyon at the monument's north end. Piedras Marcadas Canyon is reached from the western terminus of Paseo del Norte. From Interstate 25, take the Paseo del Norte exit. From Interstate 40, take the Coors Road exit and go north on Coors Road, which becomes NM 448, for 5.7 miles. Then turn left beneath the Paseo del Norte overpass toward Paradise Hills. From the end of Paseo del Norte turn right on Eagle Ranch, then left on Paradise. Follow Paradise uphill 0.7 mile to its intersection with Golf Course. Because the land adjoining Petroglyph National Monument is being developed rapidly, permanent access to Piedras Marcadas Canyon has yet to be determined. Before your visit, call the Petroglyph National Monument Visitor Center (505-899-0205) for current information. This portion of the monument is undeveloped, without interpretive markers. Farther to the south, off Unser Boulevard, which is reached by following signs on North Coors Road, is a site where the National Park Service has developed paved trails and interpretive markers and provides rangers to answer questions. Be sure also to visit the Petroglyph National Monument Visitor Center, also located on Unser Boulevard.

At Piedras Marcadas Canyon the walking is easy as you hike, and the soft sand readily records the tracks of birds and animals—coyotes, roadrunners, rabbits, squirrels, lizards, and even insects, such as the black pinacate beetles, which shove their bottoms into the air when approached. Many of these creatures you're likely to see on this trip. Contrast the ephemeral traces in the sand with those on the rocks.

As you near the escarpment, begin looking for petroglyphs. Children can make a game of finding them. Equally fun is trying to guess what the figures represent. A zigzag line, for example, could mean a river, such as the Rio Grande, or a snake or lightning. Some of the faces are thought to depict kachinas, the spirits represented by masked figures that appear in religious ceremonies of the Pueblo Indians. And it's been suggested that groups of signs tell a story. Perhaps you and your children could make up one that would fit the figures.

But also remind children that while the petroglyphs here are abundant, they face severe threats from humans. Some people have even used the petroglyphs for target practice! There's also the problem of graffiti; officials at the park are using dark pigments to obscure the work of modern vandals.

The Indians created the petroglyphs by using hand-held stones to peck at the black surface of the boulders. This dark sheen is called "desert varnish" and is the result of a complex process involving rainwater, sun, and microorganisms. The underlying volcanic rock is

Examining ancient Indian carvings in Petroglyph National Monument

a light gray, which the pecking exposed. Because the petroglyph outlines began acquiring desert varnish again as soon as they were exposed, archaeologists can use their color to estimate which are oldest. Ask children if they can detect color differences among the petroglyphs.

Once inside Piedras Marcadas Canyon, explore at will along the escarpment, but beware of the razor-sharp edges on some rocks. Though the canyon is accessible in all seasons, spring is especially pleasant, when the mesa wildflowers are in bloom and temperatures are still cool.

And as you're exploring, perhaps you and your children could glance occasionally to the east, to the modern metropolis that is Albuquerque, and imagine how the Rio Grande Valley would have appeared to the petroglyph makers who came here hundreds of years ago.

36. Phoenician Inscription Rock

Type: Dayhike
Difficulty: Easy to moderate for children
Hikable: Year-round
One way: 0.5 mile or 1.5 miles
Starting elevation: 5,050 feet
High point: 5,200 feet or 5,527 feet
Maps: Rio Puerco and South Garcia
SE 7.5-minute USGS quads
Hazards: None

The property that includes this site is now owned by Isleta Pueblo. Outsiders still can visit the site, but because it includes sites of religious significance to the pueblo's members, they insist that visitors call tribal police at 505-869-3030 to arrange to be met at the site by a ranger, who will unlock the gate. This rock with the strange writing is one of New Mexico's most persistent and best-loved mysteries. It's often called Mystery Rock but more usually Phoenician Inscription Rock because some of the characters resemble those in the Phoenician alphabet. However, the message inscribed here has never been satisfactorily deciphered, though dozens of attempts have been made. Most likely the inscription is a hoax, although the identities of the hoaxers and their motives also remain a mystery, especially as this rock hardly is in a place that normally would attract attention.

The rock is in a shallow gully on the northeast side of Hidden Mountain, a volcanic pile west of Los Lunas. It's reached by taking the Los Lunas exit from Interstate 25 and driving west on NM 6 for

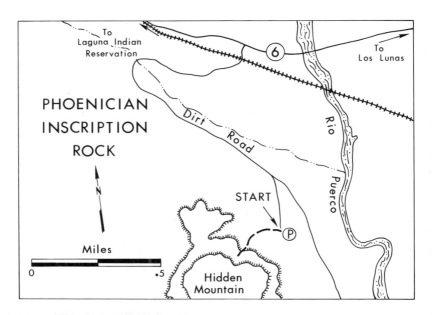

What could these characters mean? And who wrote them?

14.7 miles. Soon after crossing the Rio Puerco and just before entering the Laguna Indian Reservation, you will see a dirt road that branches left. It crosses the railroad tracks, then angles right, heading west. Almost immediately after crossing a usually dry streambed, the dirt road bends left and heads southeast, to go along the northeast side of Hidden Mountain. There are no signs indicating the way, but stick to the main dirt road and go left after the streambed. After 1.2 miles from the highway, a smaller dirt track branches right from the main dirt road and leads 0.2 mile to a fence with a crude gate; park here.

Just on the other side of the gate, a path parallels the fence before angling left to begin going up a small gully, in which are found the rock and its mysterious inscription. Some people have translated it as the Ten Commandments, perhaps carved by early Mormon immigrants. One person claimed it was inscribed by an ancient Greek named Zakyneros, wandering North America long before even the Vikings came here. In his message, Zakyneros laments his exile from his homeland—the humiliation, hunger, and hardship he endures—but doesn't mention how he got here or why he chose to write upon the rock.

But others have said the writing doesn't mean anything and the characters were invented by a hoaxer. These people point out that early persons living and traveling in the area don't mention the existence of the inscription, though it could easily have been overlooked.

But why would anyone, even a hoaxer, labor long hours to create an inscription at such an inconspicuous, out-of-the-way place?

After a break to ponder this question, continue to the top of Hidden Mountain, following faint trails that continue up either side of the gully. The hiking is steep and rocky, but the distance is short, and the views of the Rio Puerco Valley from the mountain's top are spectacular.

You'll also discover that the inscription rock is not the only mystery on this peculiar mountain. At its top are petroglyphs and the remains of dwellings created by ancient Indians. Again the question arises—why so much activity here?

Perhaps your children's imaginations will come closer to the hidden truth of Hidden Mountain.

---

37. Fourth of July Canyon

Type: Dayhike
Difficulty: Moderate for children
Hikable: April through October
One way: 2.25 miles
Starting elevation: 7,600 feet
High point: 8,690 feet
Maps: Manzano Mountain Wilderness (Cibola National Forest); Bosque Peak 7.5-minute USGS quad
Hazards: None

It all begins with a single layer of cells forming in a leafstalk and blocking the nutrient flow to the leaf. Eventually the leaf's green

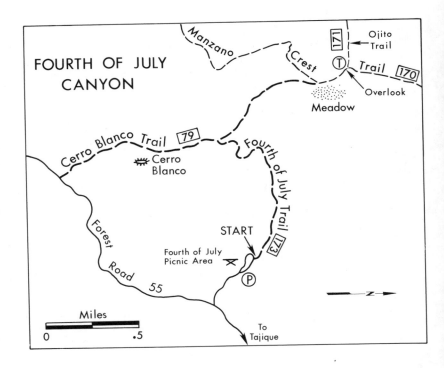

FOURTH OF JULY CANYON

chlorophyll breaks down, and if the leaf is on a Rocky Mountain maple tree, the leaf's underlying red pigment is briefly revealed before the leaf dies and falls.

Multiplied by millions, the result is one of New Mexico's most spectacular natural displays—and among its rarest, for Rocky Mountain maple is uncommon in the state, and dense stands are rarer still. Yet it happens every fall in the canyons around Fourth of July campground in the eastern Manzano Mountains.

The campground is reached by taking either Interstate 40 or NM 333 east from Albuquerque to Tijeras, then driving 29.6 miles south on NM 337 and then west on NM 55 for 3.1 miles to the old Hispanic village of Tajique. At the village's south end, Forest Road 55 heads west 7.5 miles into the Manzano Mountains foothills to the campground. This is crowded on weekends, especially during fall foliage season. The leaves' reputation is widely known, particularly among artists and photographers. At the back of the campground is Fourth of July Trail 173, marked by a sign.

The trail ascends steadily but gently up the narrow shady canyon past several springs. The maples are abundant here; children can collect leaves or play in the leafy carpet. Rare will be the child who returns from this hike without a few large maple leaves as souvenirs. Indeed, this would be a good excuse for children to make a leaf collection; if you don't have a plant press, simply bring a thick magazine or catalog between whose pages the leaves can be protected until you return home. The Rocky Mountain maples are spectacular, but they're only one of many interesting plant species here—oaks, willows, pines, and numerous wildflowers from asters to wild strawberries.

After 1.5 miles the trail joins the Cerro Blanco Trail 79. Follow this 0.5 mile north to the Manzano Crest Trail 170, then continue north on this 0.25 mile to a saddle where a sign directs you to the Ojito Trail 171, just 140 feet away.

At this junction an overlook offers a spectacular view of the Rio Grande Valley far below. Looking down, you'll see patches of red in some of the canyons, indicating the presence of more Rocky Mountain maples. To the north is limestone-banded 9,509-foot Mosca (Spanish for "fly") Peak. This overlook and the grassy meadow just to the east are delightful picnic sites. This meadow also would be excellent as an overnight campsite, though cattle often graze here and leave their droppings (perhaps that's the origin of the name Mosca!).

You could return to the campground as you came, but if you can spare a little more time and energy you'll be well rewarded to return to the 173-79 trail junction and then continue south on the Cerro

Looking north along the crest of the Manzano Mountains

Blanco Trail 79. This skirts around the west side of Cerro Blanco (Spanish for "white hill"), a small knob from whose sparsely vegetated sides you can see a panorama of the eastern Manzanos. In the fall, the maples, oaks, and other trees paint a colorful patchwork of red, yellow, green, and brown.

The Cerro Blanco Trail then descends into a small canyon and soon puts you back on Forest Road 55. The Fourth of July campground is still about 1 mile down this road to the north, but the walking is easy, and the maples here are as colorful as anywhere.

The round-trip hike is about 4.5 miles and can easily be done in 4 to 5 hours. But don't hurry this hike. The Fourth of July campground was named because local people once held Independence Day celebrations here. Now the human fireworks are elsewhere, but nature's pyrotechnics continue, quieter but no less spectacular.

Note: This hike is best during fall foliage season, but it's delightful at other seasons as well—and much less crowded.

38. Spruce Spring and Red Canyon

Type: Dayhike or backpack
Difficulty: Moderate to difficult for children
Hikable: May through October
One way: 3.4 miles
Starting elevation: 7,960 feet
High point: 9,160 feet
Maps: Manzano Mountain Wilderness (Cibola National Forest); Torreon, Capilla Peak, Manzano Peak, and Punta de Agua 7.5-minute USGS quads
Hazards: None

From your campsite at the Manzano Crest you can look out at night and see the lights of Albuquerque, Belen, and, far to the north, Santa Fe, while overhead in the clear New Mexico sky shine even the faintest stars. This, along with a moderately long but relatively easy trail, argues for doing the Spruce Spring Trail as an overnighter rather than a dayhike, for spending the night here will enhance the sense of being in the wilderness. The trail begins at the Cibola National

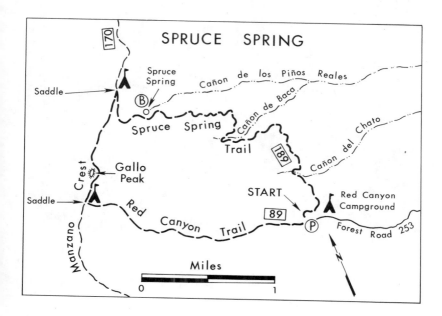

Forest Red Canyon Campground. This is reached from Albuquerque by driving east on Interstate 40 to the Tijeras exit, then taking NM 337 south 29.6 miles to NM 55. Go west on NM 55 through the old Hispanic villages of Tajique and Torreon for 12.4 miles to the seventeenth-century village of Manzano, which is Spanish for "apple," so named for orchards here. From this village the name spread to be applied also to the mountains to the west. At the junction of NM 55 and NM 131 is a sign indicating that Manzano Mountains State Park (hike 39) is 3 miles away over Forest Road 253; Red Canyon Campground is 6 miles away.

The Spruce Spring Trail 189 heads north from the campground and is marked by a sign. It ascends gradually as it passes through a forest of piñons, ponderosas, and alligator junipers. From openings in the forest are spectacular views to the east of the Estancia Valley, once filled by the huge Lake Estancia. Ask children to imagine viewing a vast sea in what now appears desert. A few shallow, saline lakes are all that remain.

Still heading north, the trail passes through Cañon del Chato and continues north until at about 1.5 miles it swings west. Its gradients remain easy, however, as it follows the hillside above Cañon de Baca and later Cañon de los Piños Reales.

Along the trail have children notice the numerous gambel oaks, with oak-shaped leaves and rough, grayish bark, often occurring in

Daisies blooming in gravelly mountain soil

dense thickets. Gambel oaks are characteristic plants of this life zone. They're an important browse plant for deer, and their acorns were eaten by Indians, who preferred them to those of other species because they're less bitter. (Children who taste them likely will disagree!) The Indians would grind the acorns into meal, leach out the bitter tannic acid with water, then mix the meal with cornmeal to make soup, bread, and pancakes. Ask children to contrast this with the breakfasts they usually eat.

Just past the 3-mile marker, a spur trail branches right 100 yards down to Spruce Spring. Formerly developed, the spring has deteriorated, though it still is a relatively reliable source of water. However, don't drink without purifying it first.

Though camping is possible at the spring, better sites are just 0.4 mile farther, where Trail 189 reaches a saddle and the junction with Manzano Crest Trail 170, marked with a sign. Immediately north of the junction are several obvious campsites that are among the most appealing in the Manzano Mountains. The small meadows interspersed with towering ponderosa pines are delightful, and from the crest are expansive views of the Rio Grande Valley as well as the northern Manzanos. This is a good place for you and your children to look for signs of wildlife.

From the saddle, follow the Crest Trail south 0.75 mile, then take a side trip to climb 10,003-foot Gallo Peak. The route to the top is faint and probably will involve some trial and error, but the distance is only about 0.5 mile, and the 360-degree views from the bare summit are truly spectacular. Curiously, this summit has on it plants, such as cacti, one doesn't expect to find at such high elevations. When last

I was here I even encountered a horned toad! Gallo is Spanish and means "rooster," but to the Spanish-speaking people of New Mexico it also has meant "wild turkey," and the forests here are indeed good habitat for these elusive birds.

After you've descended from Gallo Peak, a 0.25-mile hike farther south along Crest Trail 170 brings you to another saddle, with campsites, and the junction with Red Canyon Trail 89. This leads downhill 2.7 miles back to the Red Canyon Campground, completing the loop.

As you hike down Red Canyon, you might notice that the lushly vegetated canyon is conspicuously green, not red. Perhaps a red rock formation or red soil is visible when vegetation is not present. About a mile from the campground you'll be treated to two small but pleasant waterfalls, unless a period of drought has deprived them of water.

This trip is especially appealing in the fall, when the aspens turn a shimmering yellow and the Rocky Mountain maples a vibrant red. The Manzano Mountains are much larger and wilder than their cousins to the north, the Sandia Mountains. This hike offers people with children an excellent opportunity to have a true wilderness adventure—but with relatively short distances and modest hiking.

39. Manzano Mountains State Park

Type: Dayhike
Difficulty: Easy for children
Hikable: April through November
Round-trip: 0.5-mile to 1.75-mile loops
Starting elevation: 6,950 feet
High point: 7,400 feet
Map: Punta de Agua 7.5-minute USGS quad
Hazards: None

No one would come here for a wilderness experience, and the scenery and hiking are not among New Mexico's most spectacular, but Manzano Mountains State Park is an interesting and scenic drive from Albuquerque, and the park's network of very easy trails is a good place to introduce young children to New Mexico's most common and arguably most important life zone—the piñon-juniper forest. There are also a campground, picnic area, and a playground.

To reach Manzano Mountains State Park from Albuquerque, drive

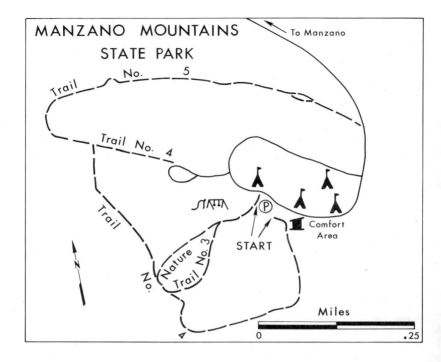

east on Interstate 40 to the Tijeras exit, then take NM 337 south 29.6 miles to NM 55. Go west on NM 55 through several old Hispanic villages such as Tajique and Torreon. These date from the seventeenth century, when the Spaniards established missions and settlements at Indian pueblos. They were called the "Saline Pueblos" because of their proximity to the salt deposits at the shallow evaporative lakes just to the east (see **Note** below). After 12.4 miles you reach the village of Manzano, named for its orchards; manzano is Spanish for "apple." At the junction of NM 55 and NM 131 is a sign indicating that Manzano Mountains State Park is 3 miles away on NM 131.

Within the park the trailheads are located at the comfort area, also the site of the playground. The nature trail is just 0.5 mile long and loops back to its start. A 1.75-mile hike can be made from here by starting on Trail 4. This heads south, then west, and eventually connects with Trail 5 to loop around the entire state park, though it can be shortened at several points by taking other trails back to the campground.

You'll notice several of the trees have been scarred by fire. Explain to children that fire no longer is regarded as a destructive evil in nature but rather as part of the natural cycle, and that some species of plants would actually die out if there were no fires. Have children look for young trees growing in open areas. Explain that if fire didn't occasionally create clearings, some tree species could never grow.

Deer are common here; have children look for their tracks in the soft soil. And point out the trees and their importance to the area's ecology: shrub live oak and gambel oak, whose leaves and acorns are important for wildlife; piñon pine, the state tree, whose nuts are eaten by animals, birds, and humans; and one-seed junipers and alligator junipers, whose seeds and twigs also are important wildlife food. Let children pick the gray-green juniper berries and taste them. Then tell the children the Indians once made a flour by grinding these berries. The Ute Indians even pulverized the shaggy bark into a soft fabric they used as diapers for their babies. Children won't have difficulty imagining how alligator juniper got its name after looking at the fine specimens here.

Remind children also that lumber from the ponderosa pines and firewood from the piñons and junipers have supported human habitation in New Mexico for thousands of years—and in the mountain villages continue to do so. Gathering piñon nuts still is an important family activity, and in the winter the air is fragrant with the distinctive scents of wood stoves burning logs from these two trees. Through-

The bark of the appropriately named alligator juniper

out much of rural New Mexico, life is inextricably linked with the piñon-juniper forest, well displayed at this state park.

Note: Since you've already driven this far, consider driving 5 more miles south on NM 55 and then another 2 miles to Quarai at Salinas Pueblo Missions National Monument, which preserves the ruins of the seventeenth-century Spanish mission built at one of the Saline Pueblos.

40. Trigo Canyon

Type: Dayhike
Difficulty: Moderate to difficult for children
Hikable: May through October
One way: 4 miles
Starting elevation: 6,250 feet
High point: 8,800 feet
Maps: Manzano Mountain Wilderness (Cibola National Forest); Capilla Peak 7.5-minute USGS quad
Hazards: None

Most hikers focus on the 25-foot waterfall here, but it's the numerous smaller waterfalls and pools along the route that truly epitomize the charm of Trigo Canyon. The trail for the most part is not very steep, at least to the waterfall, and there's plenty along the way to keep children interested.

To reach the canyon, drive south on NM 47 from its intersection with NM 309 east of Belen. At 5.8 miles at a Cibola National Forest sign, a good dirt road, Forest Road 33, passes between two adobe pillars and heads east toward the Manzano Mountains. At 5.8 miles from the highway, the dirt road bends north; then at 12.2 miles from the highway, it bends east again. At 18.6 miles the National Forest boundary is reached. At 19 miles is the former John F. Kennedy campground, now without facilities, and the trailhead.

Trigo Canyon Trail 185 is unmarked, but it's easy to find at the campground's east end, at the canyon's mouth. The trail passes through an iron gate, crosses the intermittent stream, and heads up the canyon through a forest containing numerous large alligator junipers (the bark explains the name). If you camp or picnic here, children will quickly discover these trees were made for climbing. The wide and

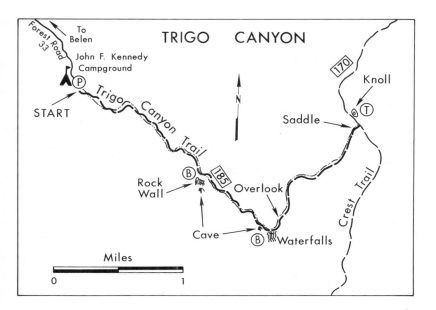

gentle path crosses the stream often as it ascends the canyon, gradually becoming narrower and rougher as towering, jagged cliffs crowd the canyon.

At about 1.5 miles, the trail passes beneath a large rock wall, just before crossing the stream. Here's a good place to break, especially as just on the up-canyon side of the wall is a very short spur trail leading right to a shallow cave that children will want to explore (watch for poison ivy). Once when my daughter and I visited the cave, we found a bat inside, hanging upside down. If you happen to encounter a bat, both you and the bat will have a better experience if you don't disturb it.

From the rock wall, the trail continues to parallel the stream

A shelf fungus

up the canyon. At about 2.5 miles, where the canyon intersects another, larger rock wall, the trail passes in front of a second shallow cave where people have camped. This also is a good breaking spot, particularly because several small waterfalls and the larger waterfall are just upstream. Children will love exploring here, climbing on the rocks and wading in the stream. Most parties, especially those whose energies are flagging, will choose to go no farther, for above the waterfall the trail becomes much steeper, switchbacking up the canyon's north side. But do go beyond the waterfall far enough to reach an overlook of the dramatic cliffs. Like most waterfalls in New Mexico, it is much more exciting in spring and early summer; by fall it's often reduced to a trickle.

Above the waterfall, the trail changes character. It still parallels a tiny stream, but instead of threading up a deep canyon it meanders up a pleasant forested valley. Fungi are abundant, especially on dead and decaying trees. (Remember: No one should ever taste any wild fungus.)

At about 4 miles you finally leave the stream and pass briefly through dry ponderosa forest before topping out at a saddle and the junction with Crest Trail 170. Just north along this trail is a pleasant knoll with beautiful views to the north. The major summit in the foreground is Osha Peak, while in the distance can be seen the towers of the Capilla Peak electronic site.

Trigo Canyon is delightful in all its seasons—spring, when the waterfalls are ripe; summer, when the wildflowers are in their glory; and fall, when the willows, woodbine, and oak turn yellow, red, and brown. Perhaps you and your children can make a game of collecting leaves according to their colors. This hike deserves all the leisure you can give it.

Western New Mexico

"Hoodoos" in the Bisti Wilderness

41. The Bisti Wilderness

Type: Dayhike
Difficulty: Easy for children
Hikable: April through November
One way: Varies
Starting elevation: 5,770 feet
High point: About 5,800 feet
Maps: Bisti Trading Post and Alamo Mesa West 7.5-minute USGS quads
Hazards: None

Bisti comes from the Navajo word meaning "badlands," and indeed this region of barren, weirdly eroded formations is "bad" for agriculture and ranching. But for geologists, paleontologists, photographers, hikers, and especially children, the Bisti is a delight. It's a place of constant discovery—strange mushroom rocks, grotesque formations called "hoodoos," glittering calcite crystals, petrified logs, and softly contoured polychrome earth formations.

The Bisti is accessible from Farmington by driving south on NM 371 for about 30 miles, then exiting left for 6 miles on a gravel road that leads past the Old Bisti Trading Post to an undeveloped parking area and wilderness access. The area also can be approached from Crown Point to the south by taking NM 371 north about 46 miles and following the same gravel road. There are no water or toilet facilities at the parking area.

The barrenness that gives the Bisti Wilderness its unique character also creates its unique challenges. The hiking is easy, but the Bisti is extremely exposed; when the sun is directly overhead, the heat and light can be intense, with no shade or water anywhere. Early morning and late afternoon are the best times for exploring. And the lack of vegetation means that windstorms can fill the air with dust; thus, fall is the best season to explore the Bisti.

While you're preparing to hike might be a good time to tell children the fascinating story about how these badlands were created. It's a story that began tens of millions of years ago, during the age of the dinosaurs. Challenge children to imagine the present dry, barren landscape as it existed then—a hot, steamy swamp, lush with vegetation, with extensive mud flats bordering a shallow sea. Ask them to picture the leaves of giant ferns parting to let pass a group of huge, horned dinosaurs, ceratopsians; their fossilized bones have been found here. Ask children to visualize the tiny creatures, first appearing about sixty million years ago, that became mammals. Their bones also are here. Fossils such as these have made the San Juan Basin among the nation's premier paleontological sites, and while you may not find dinosaur bones you'll have no trouble finding the remains of the ancient forest, including fossilized logs.

The hiking begins at the BLM parking area, but while an old road heads east along the north side of the wash, the more interesting formations are on the wash's south side, so cross over and then head east. There are no trail or other route markers, and the little ravines branch chaotically; parties with children should stay together. Also, discourage children from disturbing the fragile crust atop many formations; this crust is the product of long years of alternate wetting and drying, heating and cooling.

But do try to find opportunities for children to roam and explore. The ground often glitters with calcite crystals, and fossilized logs, complete with roots and branches, protrude from the earth. If anyone in your party is a photographer, be patient with him or her, as the unique colors and contours beg to be photographed. And this is a

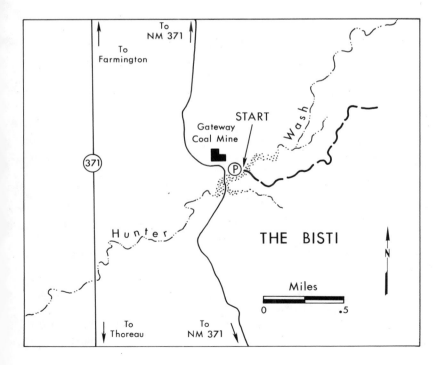

wonderful place for fantasy; my younger daughter and I concocted a tale here whose unraveling lasted for days.

As you hike, be mindful of the long, slow patience of geologic time that created this landscape, and perhaps let it remind you to slow down as well. The Bisti is not a place for hurrying or logging miles. There's too much to explore, too many reasons to pause, to wonder. Everyone's a child here.

42. Peñasco Blanco Ruins—Chaco Canyon

Type: Dayhike
Difficulty: Easy for children
Hikable: April through November
One way: 2.2 miles
Starting elevation: 6,115 feet
High point: 6,175 feet
Map: Kin Klizhin Ruins and Pueblo Bonito 7.5-minute USGS quads
Hazards: High water during thunder-showers

Chaco Canyon is a hauntingly beautiful place, and this hike to an isolated, ruined village is a good way for adults and children to get to know it, walking a route that would have been followed by the Ancestral Puebloans and their children 800 years ago.

Chaco Canyon is reached from the north by turning onto County Road 7900 3 miles east of Nageezi, approximately 50 miles northwest of Cuba. From the turnoff, which is well-marked, it is 21 miles to the park, on pavement and good dirt. From the south, turn north onto NM 371 from I-40 at Thoreau and drive to Crownpoint. Two miles north of Crownpoint, turn east on Navajo 9 and continue to a marker turnoff heading north. From here, it's 21 unpaved miles to the park.

Chaco Canyon is a very long drive from Albuquerque or Santa Fe, and while you can visit the park in one long day, you'll have a richer experience if you stay overnight. The National Park Service has a campground in Chaco Canyon near the visitor center, but space is limited; call ahead for availability of sites. No other campgrounds or

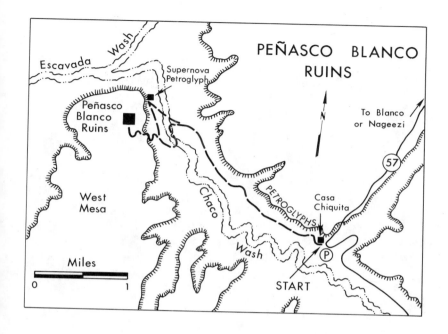

lodgings are located in—or even near—the park. Before you begin this hike, be sure to stop by the visitor center; the information there will greatly enrich your experience.

The hike to Peñasco Blanco—"white rocky outcrop"—begins north of Pueblo Bonito—"attractive town"—and goes past Pueblo Chiquita—"pretty little house." The trail follows an old road northwest along Chaco Wash, past an escarpment on whose vertical faces are numerous petroglyphs. At 0.75 mile and marked by a sign is a particularly fine Ancestral Puebloan petroglyph panel, 30 feet high on the cliff face, showing a human figure, a bighorn sheep, and a rectangular design. Bighorn sheep no longer live anywhere near Chaco Canyon; ask children why the Ancestral Puebloans might have made this carving.

All along the rock face here are petroglyphs—mostly Ancestral Puebloan but also Navajo and Mexican and, sadly, modern graffiti. Children and adults will love looking for the figures and guessing what they might depict and mean. Some people have suggested several pictures together tell a story. It might be fun for the members of your party each to make up a story using a group of petroglyphs.

As you hike in the soft sand of the route, you're very likely to encounter at least one pinacate beetle. These are large, jet-black beetles that elevate their rear ends when approached. They can eject a foul-

Masonry walls at Casa Chiquita Ruins in Chaco Canyon National Historical Park

smelling substance but otherwise are harmless, and children love watching them.

After about 1.75 miles the trail leaves the cliffs to cross Chaco Wash. Do not attempt to cross when the water's up; it can be cold, swift, and deceptively deep.

Just before the wash is a cairn-marked trail to the right leading across the wash 0.5 mile to another petroglyph site; a star-shaped figure here is thought to depict a supernova visible in 1054. This trail quickly loops back to the main trail.

The main Peñasco Blanco Trail climbs over rock ledges up West Mesa to Peñasco Blanco. This so-called "great house" village, with an unusual oval shape, was three stories high, indicating at least 160 rooms. It was inhabited from circa 913 until the general abandonment of Chaco Canyon in the 1100s. The site is unexcavated, and the fragile walls are easily damaged by people crawling over them.

While you're at Peñasco Blanco, talk to your children about Chaco Canyon and the mysteries and lessons it presents. In New Mexico Spanish, the word *chaco* means "desert," and that certainly describes the arid, treeless country around Chaco Canyon, so why did this become the site of the greatest Indian civilization north of Mexico? Scientists say the climate was not significantly wetter then—how might the environment have been different in other ways? Perhaps the water table was higher in Chaco Wash, or the vegetation was different. Most puzzling of all, what caused the Chacoans to abandon the stone communities they had labored so hard to build? Numerous theories have been advanced—drought, warfare, overpopulation, depletion of resources—but none has proved completely satisfactory. And where did the Chacoans go? Without doubt at least some of their descendants are alive today, living among the Hopi, Zuni, and the modern Pueblo Indians at Acoma, Laguna and along the Rio Grande, but there's surely much more to this story than we're aware of now.

As you hike back from Peñasco Blanco, you and your children can try to imagine that you're going not to your car but to a ceremony at Pueblo Bonito, greatest of the Chaco settlements, perhaps a ceremony of farewell, before you and all your people pack your belongings and depart forever, never suspecting that 800 years later the ruins of your homes will be visited by people very unlike yourselves.

43. Tsin Kletzin Ruins—Chaco Canyon

Type: Dayhike
Difficulty: Easy to moderate for children
Hikable: April through November
One way: 1.5 miles
Starting elevation: 6,150 feet
High point: 6,658 feet
Maps: Pueblo Bonito 7.5-minute USGS quad
Hazards: None

Tsin Kletzin, a ruined Ancestral Puebloan village atop South Mesa, is, along with Peñasco Blanco, one of the easiest backcountry hikes from Chaco Canyon, following a route that would have been trodden by Indian families centuries ago. And while small children won't necessarily understand or appreciate the archaeological significance of the ruins, older children are more likely here than elsewhere to sense

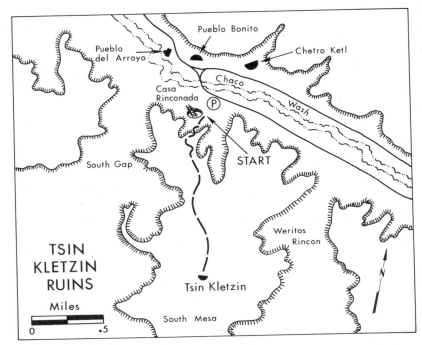

An entrance to the Great Kiva at Casa Rinconada Park

the mystery and magic of what remains of the Chacoan civilization, greatest of all the prehistoric Indian civilizations in North America north of Mexico.

Chaco Canyon is reached from the north by turning onto County Road 7900 3 miles east of Nageezi, approximately 50 miles northwest of Cuba. From the turnoff, which is well-marked, it is 21 miles to the park, on pavement and good dirt. From the south, turn north onto NM 371 from I-40 at Thoreau and drive to Crownpoint. Two miles north of Crownpoint, turn east on Navajo 9 and continue to a marker turnoff heading north. From here, it's 21 unpaved miles to the park. The park is in a very isolated part of the state, and visiting it requires considerable driving. If possible, plan to spend at least two days exploring Chaco Canyon and its many ruins. The National Park Service has a campground in Chaco Canyon near the visitor center, but space is limited; call ahead for availability of sites. No other campgrounds or lodgings are located in—or even near—the park. Before you begin the hike, be sure to stop by the visitor center; the information there will greatly enrich your experience.

This hike begins near Casa Rinconada—"house in a corner"—south of Chaco Wash. Spend a few moments at the great kiva; now partially reconstructed, it's among the largest in the Ancestral Puebloan world. Kivas are ceremonial chambers, usually circular and built underground, where members of religious societies gathered for meetings and rituals. Kivas are ubiquitous at Ancestral Puebloan sites throughout the Southwest—many villages had several—and their presence today among Pueblo Indians in New Mexico is a reminder of the cultural links between the Ancestral Puebloans and what many believe are their descendants. Ask children to imagine being in the great kiva 900 years ago; then it would not have been quiet and open to the sky as now but covered, dark, filled with smoke from torches and fires, and noisy with the sounds of drums and chanting.

The Tsin Kletzin Trail begins at Marker 9, just south of the great kiva. The trail immediately ascends the steep, rocky slope to the mesa top, from whose rim are good views of the canyon and the ruins it contains. Let children lead here, scouting for the cairns marking the route over rock ledges. Junipers like those growing here were used by the Ancestral Puebloans for firewood and construction, while the bark of cliff rose was used for baskets. The trail continues ascending gently but persistently, the sandstone becoming soft sand, until the ruins of Tsin Kletzin are reached.

Tsin Kletzin—Navajo for "charcoal place"—was built on a D-shaped plan and contained seventy rooms, with two two-story kivas in the northern section. Tree rings in roof beams give a construction date of 1112.

Tsin Kletzin, with its expansive views, intersects several lines of sight connecting other Ancestral Puebloan villages, a factor that apparently was important to the Ancestral Puebloans. From atop the highest kiva here, the ruins of Kin Klizhin, Bas'sa'ani, Peñasco Blanco, Kin Kletso, Casa Chiquita, and Pueblo Alto all are visible. If Tsin Kletzin were shifted 30 feet in any direction, not all of these great houses could be seen.

Why was this so important to the Ancestral Puebloans? Was it communication? And if so, by what means? This is just one of the many mysteries of the Chacoan civilization. Ask your children for their ideas.

And as you hike back through the soft sand and over the barren rock ledges, discuss with your children some of the theories explaining why the Chacoans abandoned their stone villages in the 1100s. Drought once was the most widely accepted explanation, but recently archaeologists have pointed out that construction and habitation occurred even during dry times and that the 1100s actually were a rather wet period. Did increased runoff in Chaco Wash result in arroyo cutting that dropped the water table beneath the fields? Was it overpopulation and depletion of resources, stripping the countryside of protective vegetation and leaving it exposed to erosion by late-summer thundershowers? Was it warfare or social conflict? Was it a combination of several factors? Or was it something completely beyond our conjecture? Ask your children's opinions; they're likely to be as valid as anyone's.

---

44. Zuni-Acoma Trail—El Malpais National Monument

Type:	Dayhike
Difficulty:	Difficult
Hikable:	Spring or Fall
One way:	7.5 miles
Starting elevation:	6,850 feet
High point:	About 6,865 feet
Maps:	El Malpais National Monument Zuni-Acoma Trail (available at the monument information center, 23 miles south of Grants on NM Hwy 53); Los Pilares and Arrosa Ranch 7.5-minute USGS quads
Hazards:	Sharp rocks, uneven footing

It's hard to imagine the child—or adult—who would not respond to the adventure of this hike. The terrain is bizarre—stark, black lava flows, pocked by huge sinkholes and unexpected grottoes. And while you'll be following an ancient Indian trail, you'll have to negotiate your way between cairns to find the route.

This hike is entirely within El Malpais National Monument and National Conservation Area, established by Congress in 1987. The Spanish *El Malpais* means "the badlands," but in New Mexico the

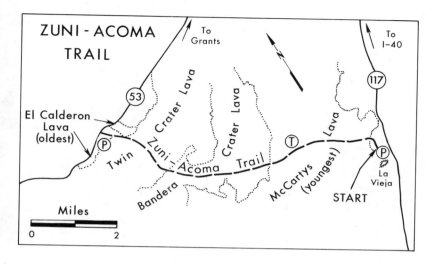

term usually refers specifically to lava flows. If you approach this hike on Interstate 40 from Albuquerque you'll pass several recent lava flows. The monument was created around the huge lava flow running many miles southwest of Grants, filling the valley with a frozen river of black rock. Many visitors assume this lava came from Mount Taylor, the 11,300-foot extinct volcano northeast of Grants that dominates the landscape in this part of the state, but in fact Mount Taylor had long been dead by the time El Malpais lava flows were created, beginning about 115,000 years ago. Indeed, El Malpais lava came not from a stereotypical volcanic cone but rather oozed from cracks in the earth, flowing through a valley carved from sandstones and limestones laid down about 260 million years ago. On the east side of the lava flow, paralleling NM 117, the sandstone cliffs are especially scenic and interesting. A great side trip is the Sandstone Bluffs Overlook, 10 miles south of Interstate 40. In wet seasons, rock pools atop the bluffs contain the tadpoles of the spadefoot toad, as well as other unusual critters, and the bluffs themselves offer great scrambling for children. This has always been among my children's favorite places.

Another good side trip for this hike is La Ventana Natural Arch, located on NM 117, 17.6 miles south of Interstate 40. For years this was believed to be New Mexico's tallest natural arch, but one in far western New Mexico recently was found to be bigger. Still, at 125 feet high and 165 feet across, La Ventana (Spanish for "the window") is very impressive. It's a short walk from the parking area to the arch.

The Zuni-Acoma Trail crosses El Malpais lava flow and runs east—west. You can do the hike in either direction, but for persons not intending to hike the entire 7.5-mile crossover, I recommend starting

Pahoehoe, *or "ropey lava," on the Zuni-Acoma Trail*

from the east. The driving distance is shorter and arguably more scenic, and the hiking distance is shorter to the younger, more dramatic lava. From Interstate 40 take the Quemado exit (Exit 89) east of Grants and drive 15 miles south on NM 117. The trailhead will be on your right, just before the striking sandstone pillar known as La Vieja (Spanish for "the old woman"). To hike from the west, exit (Exit 81) from Interstate 40 at the north end of Grants onto NM 53, then drive 18 miles south.

From the eastern trailhead, you go through an opening in the fence and then onto soft, sandy soil, but soon you're on one of the older lava flows. The trail follows the ancient route connecting the Indian pueblos of Zuni and Acoma—hence the name. Many of the cairns marking the route were built long before Europeans arrived and should not be disturbed.

After a short distance the route again enters sandy soil as it heads west. Have children look for animal tracks here; despite the harshness of the malpais environment, it nonetheless is home to a wide variety of wildlife, including coyotes, foxes, bobcats, rabbits, squirrels, mice, and more. Their tracks are easy to see in the soft sand. As late as the last century, bighorn sheep lived here; they've since vanished, victims of disease, but their horns are found occasionally. The trail here is marked by stakes, but soon it returns to lava and cairns.

There are at least four different lava flows, ranging in age from 115,000 to 3,000 years old; legends of Indian peoples still living in the area tell of rivers of "fire rock." You'll begin hiking on older lava, but soon you'll come to the abrupt and distinct boundary of the McCartys Flow, the youngest. This *pahoehoe* (pa-hoy-hoy), a Hawaiian term for "ropy lava," has numerous sinkholes and much less vegetation. Point out to children that the sparse soil on the lava has stunted the trees. Hiking on the young lava is like walking on another planet, and children will be eager to accept the responsibility of locating the cairns, which aren't always easy to spot; don't leave one cairn without having sighted the next.

Also, the lava surface is chaotic, and the rocks have extremely sharp edges. This is no place for shorts and sandals. And the lava flows are very exposed to the sun, the black mineral readily absorbing the sun's heat. Bring plenty of water, wear a hat, and if possible hike at cooler times of the day.

The McCartys Flow is about 2 miles wide; as you head west, you'll pass onto successively older flows that children will find less interesting, so linger on the younger lava and let children explore. They'll remember the hike as like no other.

45. Lava Tubes and El Calderon Crater—El Malpais National Monument

Type: Dayhike
Difficulty: Easy to moderate
Hikable: April through November
Round trip: 3-mile loop
Starting elevation: 7,277 feet
High point: 7,612 feet
Maps: El Malpais National Monument El Calderon (available at monument information center, 23 miles south of Grants on NM Hwy 53); Ice Caves 7.5-minute USGS quad
Hazards: Treacherous footing

Don't be deceived by the short hiking distance or gentle rolling terrain you'll see when you arrive here. Unless you plan to avoid the

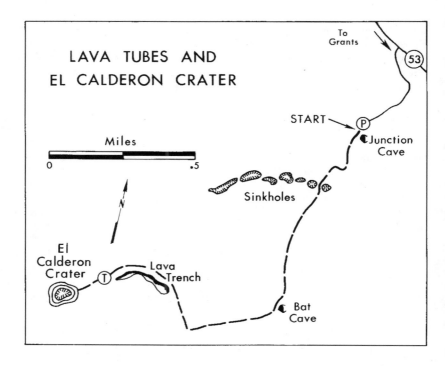

lava tubes, this trip is not for the tottery or the timid. But if you and your children relish adventure, you'll not be disappointed.

El Calderon is Spanish for "the caldron," and the name is appropriate because everywhere is evidence of the volcanism that created what is now El Malpais National Monument. As you drive here, point out to children lava flows and cinder cones; ask them to imagine the landscape when the volcanoes were erupting. Tell them they'll soon be walking beneath the lava.

To reach El Calderon, drive south on NM 53 for 20 miles from Interstate 40 at Grants. On the highway's left side a sign reading "El Calderon Area" marks a 0.25-mile gravel road to a parking area. Just south of the parking area is a collapsed lava tube; don't descend here, but from the parking area follow a well-marked trail about 100 yards east to Junction Cave.

Before descending into the darkness below, check your equipment. You need not be a trained spelunker, but you should have the following with you: tough, protective clothing; boots with gripping soles that can withstand abrasion by lava; a helmet or a hardhat; and above all, several strong, reliable sources of light. This is no place for penlights!

Within the cave, give children flashlights and let them have the excitement of leading. You'll discover the cave is much larger and longer than you expected, twisting and turning in a strange, dark world. Junction Cave is a volcanic formation known as a lava tube. Geologists tell us that these were formed when the crust of fresh lava cooled while molten lava continued to flow beneath; it's possible for surface lava to be cool enough to walk on while underneath is lava still glowing red. El Malpais National Monument includes numerous lava tubes. Most caves require a permit which must be obtained prior to your trip.

Much of the walking in the cave is over the jumbled boulders that have fallen from the ceiling, so persons with uncertain balance will have difficulty. It's possible you'll see a bat or two clinging to the cave's walls; ignore the false myths surrounding these gentle creatures, and try not to disturb them.

Eventually, the route ends at a sign barring further traffic in the cave, so retrace your steps, return to the parking lot, and take the trail leading south toward Bat Cave. After 0.25 mile you'll pass between dramatic double sinkholes. Another 0.5 mile over pleasant, open country brings you to Bat Cave. (In the fall in some years, the piñon pine trees here have edible nuts in their cones; this is a popular gathering area for Native Americans.)

Bat Cave is the home of a colony of Mexican freetail bats. In the summer, their exits from the cave can be observed at dusk from the knoll above the cave's entrance. Because bats carry diseases dangerous to humans—and to protect the bats from humans—the cave's entrance, marked by a sign, is closed to hikers. Please respect this closure. This colony has shrunk considerably in recent years, devastated by pesticides used years ago but still lingering in the soil, and disturbance by humans makes the colony's survival even more precarious.

After exploring Bat Cave, hike uphill 0.75 mile west to El Calderon Crater. There is a small dirt footpath that leads to a dirt road. Walk north on the road a short way until you see another small dirt footpath that leads to El Calderon Crater. The modest crater, nestled among ponderosa pines, is one of the oldest in the monument, but the troughs and heaps of lava all around remind us that craters such as this are very recent geologically. Children likely won't find the old volcano nearly as exciting as the caves, but they'll enjoy exploring the lava formations. Be mindful that the lava is extremely sharp, and a fall can be painful. This is no place for shorts.

From the crater, return to the dirt road and follow it back to the parking area.

46. El Morro National Monument

Type:	Dayhike
Difficulty:	Easy to moderate for children
Hikable:	April through November
One way:	2.5-mile loop
Starting elevation:	7,205 feet
High point:	7,440 feet
Map:	El Morro Trails (available at El Morro National Monument); El Morro 7.5-minute USGS quad
Hazards:	Cliffs

El Morro is Spanish and simply means "the bluff," but while that accurately labels the buff-colored formation rising abruptly from the high plain, the formation's Navajo and Zuni names better reveal its significance. They mean "writing upon rock," and for centuries Indian,

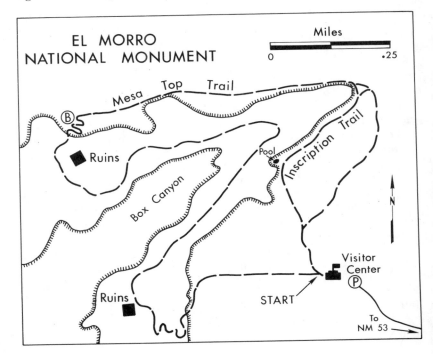

Come on up, there's plenty of room.

Spanish, and American travelers stopping for water here have paused to carve in the soft sandstone some record of their passing. Children may not be interested in the historical details behind the inscriptions, but they'll delight in spotting the faint tracings. And just when their interest is waning, there's an easy but dramatic hike to some ruins perched on the bluff's top.

To reach El Morro from Interstate 40, take exit 81 at the west end of Grants, then drive south on NM 53 for 41 miles. Most of this parallels the western edge of El Malpais National Monument, and you'll pass by numerous extinct but recent volcanoes, as well as lava fields and cinder cones. Along the route are interpretive markers reminding modern travelers that the corridor between the inhospitable lava fields and the Zuni Mountains was an ancient route for Indians traveling between Zuni and Acoma pueblos.

At El Morro National Monument, register at the visitor center and get an interpretive trail guide—you'll want it for the inscriptions—then begin the hike by following the paved, wheelchair-accessible path to the cliff's base. Here you'll find the pool whose water meant so much to the early travelers. When full, the pool is 12 feet deep and holds 200,000 gallons; the rock formation down which the water flows from the mesa above has been called "the funnel." And here, at the Inscription Trail, you'll begin finding the famed inscriptions.

The Inscription Trail is 0.5 mile of very easy walking, especially as you'll stop frequently to look at more inscriptions. The oldest and most famous of these was inscribed by Don Juan de Oñate, who led the 1598 expedition that colonized New Mexico for the Spanish and who was New Mexico's first Spanish governor. The inscription in

Spanish is *"Paso por aqui el adelantado Don Juan de Oñate del descubrimiento de la mar del sur a 16 de Abril de 1605,"* or in English, "Passed by here the Governor Don Juan de Oñate from the discovery of the Sea of the South [Gulf of California] on the 16th of April, 1605."

No one knows exactly what motivated Oñate to make the first inscription, to be followed over the centuries by so many others, but perhaps he was inspired by the petroglyphs of prehistoric Indians who stopped here. They, too, left their marks, though their meanings are far more ambiguous. One series—hand prints, footprints, and a zigzag line pointing toward a hole in the rock—has been interpreted to mean "follow the hand and foot trail to the pool of water."

As you view the inscriptions, take a moment with your children and try to capture in your imaginations some images of the earlier sojourners at El Morro. And remind yourselves that you, too, are part of that ancient tradition, that you, too, have passed by here, *"paso por aqui."*

At the bluff's northeast side, the Inscription Trail ends and a trail loops back to the visitor center, but far preferable is joining the Mesa Top Trail here. This trail, clearly labeled, heads west, following the base of the cliffs through open ponderosa forest. After about 0.5 mile the trail approaches some switchbacks; wooden benches here encourage a break to enjoy the beautiful, expansive views before climbing to the mesa's top.

Immediately upon reaching the flat summit you'll find to your left some unexcavated Indian ruins. The trail winds around these, and soon you'll be hiking over bare sandstone; the grooves and steps were cut by the National Park Service, not ancient Indians, but children will enjoy walking through them nonetheless.

Notice the box canyon enclosed by the mesa. Let children shout a few times to hear the echoes from its walls, but they should avoid the cliffs' precipitous edges.

Another 0.5 mile brings you to the ruins of another village. Once with buildings two and three stories high, this site was occupied 800 years ago. The Zuni Indians call the ruined village Atsinna, "writing upon rock." Why did the ancient Indians build here? you might ask your children. Easy to defend, with water nearby and flat stones abundantly available for construction, the site was excellent for a village. What local resources existed to support life? The box canyon would have been a good place for crops; game would have been plentiful, as well as timber. But why was the village abandoned long before the Spanish arrived? We don't really know, though it's been suggested the inhabitants moved to more fertile farmland near Zuni.

From Atsinna the trail descends to the visitor center, with several grottoes and crevices along the way for children to explore. Overnight camping is available in the monument.

47. Cebolla Creek Waterfalls

Type: Dayhike
Difficulty: Easy for children
Hikable: April through October
One way: 0.5 mile
Starting elevation: 7,020 feet
High point: 7,313 feet
Map: Ramah 7.5-minute USGS quad
Hazards: Cliffs bordering stream

Everyone in the Ramah area knows about these falls, and they say that in the spring and early summer, when the runoff is heavy from the Zuni Mountains, they are singularly beautiful. But even in late summer and fall, when the runoff—and the falls—are nonexistent, the long drive is still worth it. For children it's a very easy hike, and the dramatically sculpted rock formations are fun to explore even when the stream is dry, because potholes in the streambed contain water—and water animals.

For adults, much of this hike's appeal will lie in the scenic drive.

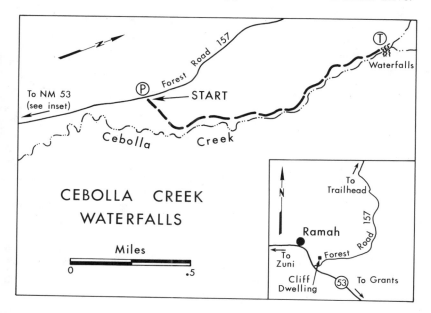

NM 53 southwest of Grants winds through the volcanic landforms of El Malpais National Monument (hikes 44 and 45) and past the dramatic, historic bluff of El Morro, also a national monument (hike 46). It's among the most scenic and historically significant landscapes in New Mexico.

To get to Cebolla (seh-BOY-yah) Creek, take NM 53 about 52 miles southwest of Grants. About 1 mile before the village of Ramah, Forest Road 157 branches right (this road also is marked by a sign for Timberlake Ranch). Forest Road 157 is a good dirt road, though it can be slick in wet weather. Numerous side roads branch from it, but 157 remains the largest road and is clearly marked. Just as you turn onto Forest Road 157 from NM 53, watch for a small cliff dwelling nestled beneath an overhang above the road's left side. If you decide to hike up to the ruins, please respect their fragility. Soon Forest Road 157 enters broad valleys flanked by towering sandstone cliffs with alternating red and white sedimentary layers. (Ask children to suggest a name for the cliffs.) At 7.6 miles, just before 157 becomes much steeper, rougher, and narrower, a small road branches right and leads across the Cebolla Valley to a rock-crushing operation. You could drive this small road 0.5 mile to within 100 yards or so of the falls, but I recommend parking on Forest Road 157 and walking the narrow road instead; the walk is short, easy, and a pleasant way to warm up before the falls.

As you walk you'll have a beautiful view down the Cebolla Valley, and you'll have no difficulty understanding the appeal this area had for the Mormon settlers who came here more than 100 years ago. Part of that appeal was Cebolla Creek, where they created a tiny settlement named Savoya. When Mormon missionaries arrived in the 1870s, the Navajo chief Jose Pino showed them the most favorable location to settle. It was in a valley the Navajos called Stinking Grass Springs. The "stinking grass" was wild onion, and the local Spanish speakers called the valley Cebolla, meaning the same thing. The Mormons anglicized the spelling to Savoya, which appeared on some maps as Savoia. Eventually, settlement shifted from Savoya to the village of Ramah down the valley. This originally had been called Navajo, for the Indians living nearby, but this name duplicated another town's name, so the name Ramah, taken from the Bible, was chosen instead. Even in late summer, when Cebolla Creek has shrunk to a trickle, you can see pools fringed with cattails and other riparian plants. Perhaps you might even find some of the wild onions—easily identified by their smell—that gave the valley its name.

The small road leading across the valley bends into the canyon and after about 100 yards the rocks of the falls' lower portion are visible. A faint trail goes along ledges on the west side of the falls, though it's possible also to walk along the stream's east side.

When the water is high, the waterfalls are truly spectacular. And when the water is low, the pools and potholes carved in the soft sandstone by the intermittent stream become visible, the rocks' intricate and convoluted contours reminiscent of the soap sculptures many of us carved as children.

I recommend following the faint trail atop the gorge's west side. Soon the first series of falls ends, but in less than 50 yards a second begins, even larger and more spectacular than the first. Here the water has actually punched holes in the rock so that a person with good balance could walk short, narrow stone bridges over water falling beneath. (I don't recommend this for children; a misstep could be disastrous.) Above in the gorge is a series of deep potholes, like beads on a string, that even in late summer are filled with water. A few of the potholes contain small fish. Are they trapped here? Or have they adapted to living part of the year in a swiftly flowing stream and the rest of the year in a stagnant pool?

Pools and potholes during the dry season on Cebolla Creek

Eventually, the rock walls constricting the stream open up, ending the waterfalls. In dry weather you can cross the stream here and return on the stream's east side.

Southern New Mexico

Approaching the west face of the Organ Mountains

48. Potato Canyon Waterfall

Type: Dayhike
Difficulty: Easy to moderate for children
Hikable: April through October
One way: 3 miles
Starting elevation: 6,750 feet
High point: 7,180 feet
Maps: Cibola National Forest,
Magdalena District; Mount
Withington 7.5-minute USGS
quad
Hazards: Flash floods

This is a trip for the adventurous. Not that the hiking is particularly challenging—in fact, it's relatively easy—but as you drive here you'll be negotiating rough dirt roads in a vast, wild, sparsely populated region of New Mexico few persons ever visit. The hike is worth it—and so is the drive.

Potato Canyon is located on the east side of the San Mateo Mountains. To get there, drive first to the former mining and cattle-drive town of Magdalena on US 60, west of Socorro. From Magdalena, two routes are possible, both leading to Forest Road 56. On the first, drive 12 miles west of Magdalena on US 60 to where NM 168, the road to Mount Withington, goes south. Drive 8.8 miles on this good dirt road to where Forest Road 52 branches left; this road is narrow and often rocky, and it's 11 miles to Forest Road 56. An easier way to reach Forest Road 56 is at the west end of Magdalena; take NM 107, a good dirt road, southwest 17.3 miles to where Forest Road 52 branches right (west). After 3.4 miles of road that's rough but nonetheless passable by passenger cars, Forest Road 56 branches left. A sign says this is a primitive road and not suited for passenger cars, but most cars should handle it if driven slowly and cautiously. Forest Road 56 leads into Big Rosa Canyon. After 2.8 miles from the 52-56 junction, you reach a sign reading "Potato Tr. No. 38." Park here to start the hike.

You'll begin by walking west on an old road, toward the mouth of Potato Canyon, but after only 0.25 mile you'll encounter the Mount Withington Wilderness boundary, where the road is replaced by a faint trail leading into the canyon. This trail is marked by blazes on trees, but if you lose the trail temporarily don't despair; the route simply follows the canyon bottom all the way to the waterfall, and you're likely to pick up the trail blazes again soon. A good strategy is to assign children the responsibility of looking for upcoming blazes.

As you walk, you might wonder why this canyon is called Potato and not *Nogal*, the Spanish word for the Arizona walnut, as the lower part of the canyon has numerous trees of this relatively uncommon desert hardwood. It was named Potato Canyon because of the huge potato-shaped boulders at the canyon's head. The other trees are what you would expect here—ponderosas, piñon, juniper, and the appropriately named alligator juniper, with its corrugated bark.

Even without a trail, the hiking is relatively easy. The canyon floor is paved with pebbles and cobbles of the fine-grained volcanics of which the San Mateo Mountains are formed. But as you hike point out to children that these rocks and the unvegetated gravel streambed are reminders that this watercourse has been scoured often by flash floods. In fact, have children look at the bases of trees to see if they can tell how high the water has risen during these floods. Have them look also at the steep, confining walls of the canyon to see how dangerous a canyon like this can be during a flash flood.

Easy as ambling along the streambed is, the route is even easier over the faint trail marked by tree blazes. Follow these to avoid any

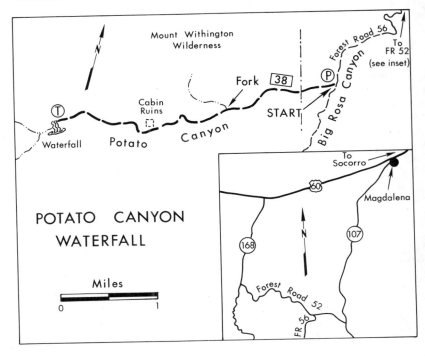

POTATO CANYON
WATERFALL

Pink Glissade, the waterfall in Potato Canyon

chance of going right instead of left at a fork at 1.25 miles. This fork is not obvious, but it appears on the maps and is mentioned in some guidebooks; stay in the main canyon and you can't go wrong.

Before long you encounter a tiny intermittent stream. At one point the trail briefly leaves the streambed and climbs over a shoulder to avoid a rockfall clogging the watercourse, but it soon drops down again. At about 2 miles, on the north side of the stream, are the decaying remains of a log cabin. Before long the canyon narrows, hemmed in by pinkish cliffs. Here the trail again leaves the streambed, but ignore the trail and instead push upstream, past a grotto formed by an overhanging wall of pinkish stone with conspicuous vertical fissures.

And there is the waterfall, the tiny stream glissading merrily down a ledge of pinkish rock into a small pool, then meandering over a bed of pale gravel. It's a beautiful, pristine place, innocent of fire rings or other signs of humans (leave it as unspoiled as you found it). Children will love splashing in the shallow pool at the fall's bottom and scrambling up the rocks into the tiny cleft where there are other little pools. The waterfall has no name (Potato Canyon Waterfall seems inappropriate for such a lovely, delicate little fall). I call it Pink Glissade, but ask your children to suggest other names.

As you drive back to US 60, consider taking a brief side trip west on the highway to the Plains of San Agustin, between Magdalena and Datil. These vast treeless plains, enclosed by wild mountains, are interesting in themselves, but they also are the site of the Very Large Array (VLA) radio telescope, operated by the National Radio Astronomy Observatory and funded by the National Science Foundation. The VLA is among the world's largest radio telescopes, and children will enjoy seeing its 27 movable white antennas, each weighing 2.5 tons and standing eerily on the vast plain like a scene from a science-fiction movie.

And as you drive back to Magdalena along US 60, tell your children of the days when this route was known officially as the Magdalena Livestock Driveway and informally as the Beefsteak Trail or the Hoof Highway. In 1919 alone, 21,677 cattle and 150,000 sheep were driven over the trail.

---

49. White Mountain Wilderness Crest Trail

Type:	Dayhike or backpack
Difficulty:	Moderate for children
Hikable:	April through October
One way:	5 miles
Starting elevation:	9,220 feet
High point:	10,400 feet
Maps:	White Mountain Wilderness (Lincoln National Forest); Angus and Nogal Peak 7.5-minute USGS quads
Hazards:	Stinging nettles along trail

In summer tourists swarm like bees in Ruidoso, but the wildflowers screen-printed on T-shirts in gift shops can be seen in reality in the White Mountain Wilderness just a few miles away. In the high

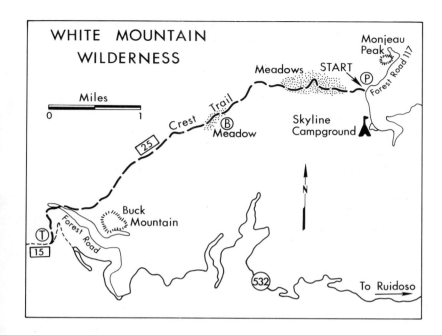

meadows, expanses of lupine give a pale blue cast to the hillside, while the 5-foot spires of green gentian resemble Chinese pagodas. Children will enjoy sniffing the abundant wild onion.

Perhaps the best of the White Mountain Wilderness trails is the Crest Trail. This goes 21.7 miles from near Monjeau Peak in the south to Nogal Peak in the north. This hike, which starts at the trail's southern end, covers only a portion of the total length. The trailhead is reached by driving north on NM 48 from Ruidoso to the little community of Alto (Spanish for "high"), then taking NM 532 west. After about a mile Forest Road 117 goes north. This steep and often rough road leads after 12 miles to the Lincoln National Forest fire lookout at 9,641-foot Monjeau Peak. It's worth the trip to allow children to climb the lookout and get an expansive view of the White Mountain Wilderness. The wilderness takes its name from 12,003-foot Sierra Blanca (Spanish for "white mountain") to the south. This mountain is sacred to the Mescalero Apaches, whose reservation includes the peak. The U.S. Forest Service Skyline Campground (no water) is about 1 mile before the lookout, and the trailhead for Crest Trail 25 is 0.5 mile before the lookout.

Trail 25 begins at about 9,220 feet and almost immediately enters the large meadows that are its main feature. Children will love discovering the dazzling variety of wildflowers here, but they should wear long pants and long-sleeve shirts because stinging nettle is among the species present. This is an excellent hike on which to play a wildflower game, such as finding the first yellow flower, the first red one, the tallest, the shortest, the most fragrant, the least fragrant, and so forth.

The pattern of mixed meadows and forest is excellent habitat for wildlife, and children will enjoy looking for signs of deer and elk. Sometimes their tracks are found along the trails, sometimes their droppings.

The trail meanders through meadows, then enters pleasant spruce-fir forest before climbing to another meadow at 2.5 miles. This is a good place for a break or to turn around.

From here the Crest Trail continues ascending gradually another 2 miles to 10,400 feet as it passes along the west side of Buck Mountain, site of electronic facilities. From there it descends to junction with Trail 15, which connects with the Ski Apache ski area.

Dayhikers will retrace their steps, while backpackers will choose a site along the Crest Trail.

---

50. White Sands National Monument

Type:	Dayhike or backpack
Difficulty:	Easy for children
Hikable:	Year-round
One way:	Varies
Starting elevation:	3,990 feet
High point:	3,990 feet
Maps:	Garton Lake and Heart of the Sands 7.5-minute USGS quads
Hazards:	Confusing topography, intense sunlight

This is the ultimate sand pile: thousands of acres of soft, snow-white sand piled into huge dunes, perfect for jumping, sliding, somersaulting, castle-building, all the things children—or adults—can do with sand.

But White Sands also is excellent hiking, and it's unlike hiking anywhere else in the world.

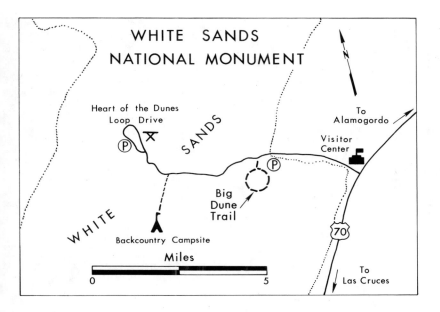

White Sands National Monument is reached by taking US 70 for 14 miles southwest of Alamogordo. (There's no car camping at the monument, but a public campground is not too distant, at Oliver Lee State Park; see hike 51.) The national monument allows backcountry camping on a permit basis at designated sites; inquire at the visitor center for their current locations. These are especially appealing on nights with a full moon. Be sure to stop at the visitor center at the monument's entrance to pick up current information and learn about the area's unique ecology.

From the visitor center drive into the heart of the dunes. At about 3 miles you'll reach the trailhead for the Big Dune Trail, a 1-mile self-guided nature trail.

Though you can stop at any of the numerous pullouts along the road, most people continue another 4 miles into the complex of parking areas known as the Heart of the Dunes, where shaded picnic sites and toilets are available. Water is not available, however. Because the steep sand slopes make excellent sliding, many parties with children take smooth plastic disks or sheets used for sliding on snow.

There are no trails; just begin hiking wherever your fancy takes you. Remember to take plenty of water, and also remember that the light and heat coming off the gleaming white dunes can be intense at midday; take sunglasses, sunscreen, and broad-brimmed hats. In the summer, late afternoons and evenings are preferable for hiking.

The real reason White Sands National Monument was established

Best of all are evenings with a full or nearly full moon, which will rise spectacularly over the Sacramento Mountains to the east.

As you hike, especially if you hike barefoot (who could resist?), you'll soon notice that though these are called "sand" dunes, the sand is nothing at all like what we usually think of as sand, which consists of tiny quartz particles. This "sand" is composed of gypsum, a much softer mineral than quartz. Tens of thousands of years ago the basin containing White Sands held a huge, totally enclosed lake, called Lake Lucero. The water of the lake contained a large amount of dissolved gypsum, which had been washed out of sedimentary formations in the San Andres Mountains to the west. About 20,000 years ago, Lake Lucero began to dry up, and as its water evaporated, small gypsum crystals precipitated out of the mineralized water. Much later, a change in weather patterns caused winds to blow over the dry lake bed (some of Lake Lucero still survives), picking up the gypsum crystals and transporting them northeasterly to deposit them in White Sands. This complex process of gypsum weathering out of the mountains, washing into Lake Lucero, precipitating as crystals, and then being blown into huge dunes continues today.

The fine grains of the gypsum sand are excellent for retaining the tracks of the insects, birds, reptiles, and animals that make White Sands their home. As you explore, have your children watch for them. Because most creatures here are most active at night, early morning is the best time to look for tracks.

As you hike at White Sands, the dunes soon will all tend to resemble each other, so unless you retrace your steps it's easy to get turned around. Try to find landmarks and keep them in sight; if nothing else, the Sacramento Mountains to the east and the San Andres Mountains to the west always are visible.

But as interesting as hiking at White Sands may be, for children the real fun is simply playing on the dunes—why not join them?

51. Dog Canyon

Type: Dayhike or backpack
Difficulty: Moderate to difficult for children
Hikable: Year-round
One way: 2.6 miles (to stone cabin)
Starting elevation: 4,415 feet
High point: 5,800 feet
Maps: Deadman Canyon and Alamogordo South 7.5-minute USGS quads
Hazards: Heat

Geronimo, while imprisoned at Fort Sill, Oklahoma, lamented that the white invaders had taken his Dog Canyon. Of all his southern New Mexico strongholds, the Apache leader was especially fond of this canyon in the west face of the Sacramento Mountains.

It's easy to see why. In a parched, treeless environment, perennial springs in the canyon's bottom offered not only water but also edible plants and welcome shade beneath giant cottonwoods and box elders. And the towering limestone cliffs flanking the canyon made for effective defense against attackers. At least five battles between the Indians and U.S. Army troops were fought in the canyon, which was named when troops came upon a hastily abandoned Apache camp here and found only a little dog. Today the Apaches have departed, and the only

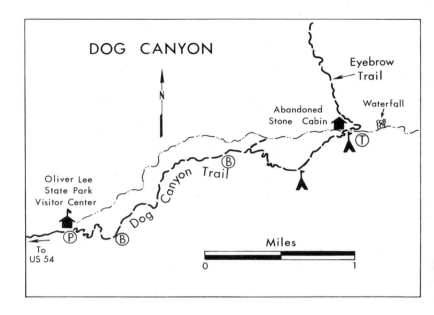

danger faced by hikers is the intense, desiccating sun. But the drama of the setting remains.

The hike into Dog Canyon begins at the Oliver Lee State Park Visitor Center, located 10 miles south of Alamogordo, 5 miles east of US 54. The park coincides with the ranch of Oliver M. Lee, one of New Mexico's most influential and controversial figures of the late nineteenth century. The outcome of his trial for murder—he was acquitted—is debated still in New Mexico. Overnight camping is available at the park, and the visitor center has historical and natural history exhibits of the canyon. A sign at the trailhead shows the route and distances as well the locations of the major battles.

Before beginning the hike, fill children's stomachs and water bottles with liquids, for the trail is very exposed, with little shade.

The trail starts by switchbacking steeply up the side of the canyon for about 0.5 mile before leveling off at the site of a peace conference between the army and the Indians. This is a good place for a water break.

About 1 mile farther into the canyon, after some more climbing, you reach another level grassy area. A battle was fought here, and as you stand surrounded by ocotillo, creosote bush, and other desert plants, ask children to imagine Indians darting about among the rocks and cliffs above, firing at soldiers seeking cover behind huge boulders.

In this level area is a cutoff trail, shown on the sign at the beginning of the hike, that leads about 0.3 mile to a spring in the canyon bottom below. If you're tired or the sun is becoming intense, this would be a good turnaround point.

If you continue on the main trail, you climb steeply for about 0.5 mile before reaching another grassy meadow just beneath towering cliffs. With a perennial stream just a short distance farther, the meadow is an obvious campsite, and where you are walking Apaches once walked also. Leaving the meadow, the trail descends 0.25 mile to a

Yucca plants and the forbidding cliffs of Dog Canyon

stream in the canyon bottom and the ruins of a stone cabin used by cowboys. Cottonwoods flanking the stream offer the first real shade since the visitor center, 2.6 miles away; the stream's pools are clear and cold—wonderful for wading.

Just up the canyon the water descends over limestone ledges in a series of waterfalls, among the most scenic in New Mexico. Several campsites are here, and it's a natural picnic site for day hikers as well. Most parties will stop here.

From the cabin, the trail begins to climb steeply out of the canyon. It's called the Eyebrow Trail here because it traverses narrow ledges arching over cliffs as it ascends the canyon's headwall.

It was here that the aged Apache chief Nana and his handful of warriors in 1880 ambushed sixty soldiers who had trailed them into Dog Canyon. When the soldiers reached the Eyebrow Trail, the Apaches rolled rocks onto the soldiers, killing or injuring most of them.

After about 1 mile from the cabin, the trail leaves the canyon and enters the grassy meadows of the Sacramento ridge. It's a good place to break before returning.

It's been more than 100 years since the Apaches battled the soldiers in Dog Canyon. But in that deep, wild solitude, among those harsh, forbidding cliffs, memories of the old conflicts still reverberate. Yet for all its tragic history, Dog Canyon is remarkably serene and beautiful. Hiking back to the visitor center at evening, remind children than the Apaches came here not for war but for refuge.

---

52. Pine Tree Trail

Type:	Dayhike
Difficulty:	Moderate for children
Hikable:	Year-round
One way:	2.25 miles
Starting elevation:	5,600 feet
High point:	6,980 feet
Maps:	Organ Peak 7.5-minute USGS quad
Hazards:	None

The Pine Tree Trail is deservedly among the most popular hiking trails in the Organ Mountains. It's not too difficult, the views are spectacular, and there's lots to interest children.

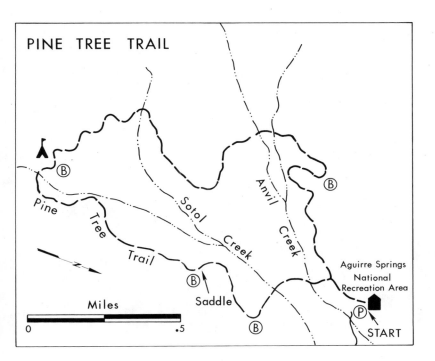

PINE TREE TRAIL

The trail starts at the Aguirre Springs National Recreation Area, managed by the Bureau of Land Management and reached by driving a paved road about 5.5 miles south of US 70 just east of San Augustine Pass. The trailhead is well-marked at the parking area.

The Pine Tree Trail is a loop trail, and after just 100 yards, in Anvil Creek, the trail splits. Either route is scenic and they both cover the same ground. Going counterclockwise (southwest instead of southeast) has a more gradual ascent. Going clockwise gives a steeper descent but puts you at a natural turnaround after only 1 mile.

At Anvil Creek point out to children the devastation caused by flash floods in the summer of 1991. Boulders as large as 18 feet long were moved by the water. Such sights should be a reminder of the danger of narrow mountain canyons during thunderstorms.

Assuming you choose the clockwise route, moving south from Anvil Canyon you cross Sotol Creek and then climb gently onto the canyon's south side. Soon you reach a series of switchbacks, the first offering a good place for a break.

Have children notice the plants along the trail here—alligator juniper, sotol, mountain mahogany, prickly pear cactus, Apache plume,

The eastern side of the Organ Mountains seen from the road to the Aguirre Springs National Recreation Area

squawbush—all common in the Upper Sonoran Desert. A particularly beautiful plant is sotol (pronounced SOH-tohl). Easily confused with yucca, it has a basal cluster of pliant, ribbonlike leaves edged with hooked thorns and a tall flower stalk of cream-colored flowers. Apache plume takes its name from the wispy, tawny tassels that form after the showy white petals have fallen away. As you climb, these will give way to gambel oak and ponderosa pine. In the soil look for the tracks of deer, coyotes, and other mammals.

From several points along the route are good views of the highest and most rugged peaks of the Organ Mountains: Sugarloaf Peak to the southeast, the Needles to the south and west, and Rabbit Ears to the northwest. Ask your children if they can tell from their shapes which mountains have these names.

After about 1 mile you reach a small saddle—an obvious place for a break, particularly as the views are spectacular. Beyond the saddle, the trail becomes distinctly rougher and steeper, nothing serious, but if any in your party are becoming weary, this is a good place to turn around. From the saddle, the trail continues 1.25 miles to reach, just after crossing a tributary of Sotol Creek, the halfway point and a primitive campsite. This is another natural place for a break in the shade of the massive ponderosa pines for which the trail likely was named.

From here the trail descends. As you cross another tributary of Sotol Creek, ask children to notice how the flash flood scoured the narrow watercourse. Notice also the spectacular views of the Organ Mountains. The descent will go rapidly, but take time occasionally to pause and look around. The plant life here is rich and diverse. This is the eastern Organs at their best.

53. Dripping Springs and Ice Canyon

Type: Dayhike
Difficulty: Easy for children
Hikable: Year-round
One way: 1.75 miles
Starting elevation: 5,660 feet
High point: 6,250 feet
Maps: Organ Peak 7.5-minute USGS quad
Hazards: None

It's easy to see why the resort Col. Eugene Van Patten built at Dripping Springs in the 1870s was so popular. It's just east of Las Cruces, in the Organ Mountains, and on hot summer days a shaded canyon with a waterfall must have been irresistible.

To reach this convenient escape from Las Cruces, continue east on University Boulevard past the Interstate 25 intersection; this road becomes the Dripping Springs Road, mostly good dirt. After about 10.5 miles past the Interstate 25 intersection it arrives at the BLM A. B. Cox Visitor Center. To reach this from US 70 just west of Organ, take the good dirt Baylor Pass Road 7 miles south. Parking and rest rooms are at the visitor center, as well as information about the area's history. The very short and interesting La Cueva hike 54 also begins at this visitor center. The well-marked Dripping Springs trail heads southeast from here into the shallow watercourse called Ice Canyon, named because sunlight rarely penetrates its upper portions.

As you walk the gently sloping trail, point out to children such desert plants as desert willow, netleaf hackberry, Apache plume, alligator juniper, yucca, sotol, and acacia. The vegetation is sparse, and

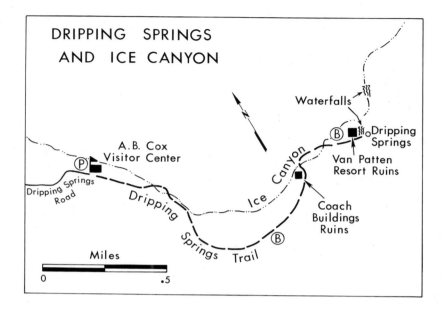

all the plants have evolved techniques for coping with the dry air and intense sun. Some have tiny, easily shed leaves; others have leaves with thick waxy coatings that prevent evaporation. Before long you'll cross the dry streambed. Ask children how often and when they think this has water in it. In an environment such as this, water is a critical concern to all travelers. It certainly was to the Apaches of southern New Mexico, who had to be familiar with all the precious few water sources in these arid mountains.

Soon the trail will veer east, offering spectacular views of the precipitous Organ Mountains. The most rugged section of these mountains, visible before you, was formed when igneous rocks intruded into sedimentary formations that created the less jagged mountains to the north and south. Benches along the way offer several opportunities to sit and enjoy the vistas.

At about 1.5 miles, the trail passes by the ruined coach buildings of Van Patten's resort. Just 0.25 mile farther you'll come to the waterfall, and just beyond this is the ruined resort. (Keep children outside the decaying building.) Van Patten, a colorful character, was a former officer in the armies of the Confederacy who settled in Las Cruces and became the Butterfield Overland Mail representative for the area. He built his fourteen-room hotel of native stone and situated it beneath an overhanging rock near the waterfall.

This is a perfect place for a picnic or just a break. Let children

The waterfalls at Dripping Springs

play around the waterfall, or continue up Ice Canyon past the resort to another small waterfall; the route is vague and the underbrush dense, but the distance is short. And ask children to imagine the resort during its heyday, when the paint was fresh, the lawn and gardens manicured, all to receive visitors brought by horse-drawn surreys.

54. La Cueva

Type: Dayhike
Difficulty: Easy for children
Hikable: Year-round
One way: 0.5 mile
Starting elevation: 5,660 feet
Ending elevation: 5,550 feet
Map: Organ Peak 7.5-minute USGS quad
Hazards: None

This is a great hike for small children—easy, short, with interesting vegetation, a cave, and even a murder mystery.

The object of the hike is a low cave (*cueva* in Spanish) in which a hermit lived—and was killed. Juan Maria de Agostini was born of noble parents in Italy around 1800, but early in life he devoted himself to religious asceticism. He immigrated to the United States and around 1863 arrived in New Mexico over the Santa Fe Trail. He began living in a cave high on a peak—now called Hermits Peak—northwest of Las Vegas, where he soon was revered by the local people for his holiness and healing abilities. But in 1867 he moved, eventually settling in this cave in the foothills of the Organ Mountains, and it was here that one day in 1869 he was found, clutching a crucifix, with a knife in his back. His murder was never solved.

The trail to his cave begins at the BLM A. B. Cox Visitor Center, also the beginning of Dripping Springs hike 53. Reach the center either by driving the good dirt Dripping Springs Road for 11 miles east from Las Cruces (continue east on University Boulevard in Las Cruces) or by taking the good dirt Baylor Pass Road 7 miles south from US 70, just west of Organ. Parking and rest rooms are available here, as well as information about the area and a guide to some of the plants you'll encounter along the trail.

The trail heads northwest from the visitor center, descending gently

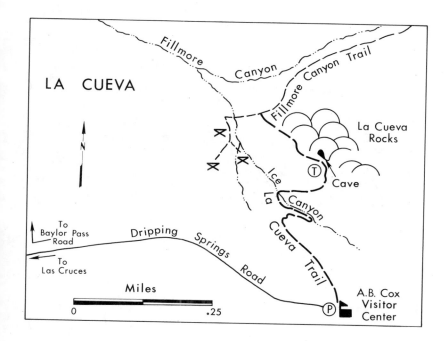

over an old road; numbered signs are keyed to the trail guide for plants. Several species of acacia are along the trail; children love discovering the appropriateness of the name cat-claw acacia. Its other common names—"tear-blanket" and "wait-a-minute"—also are appropriate. Its thorns notwithstanding, this is an important plant in the desert ecology, for its fragrant flowers, blooming in May, feed many insects, including honeybees, and the stringbeanlike fruits, ground into meal, were an important food for Indians. Rabbits and birds don't mind the cat-claw acacia's thorns at all when they retreat into thickets seeking safety from predators.

The trail dips briefly into cool and shady Ice Canyon, named for its sunless upper reaches, just before ascending to the cave over a slab of rock in which are several "potholes" used by ancient Indians as mortars. Ask children to imagine sitting here while their mothers ground corn for the family's meals. Quite a contrast to going to the supermarket!

Children will enjoy exploring the shallow cave. Point out the smoke-stained ceiling and ask them to imagine the hermit cooking his evening meal here. Local lore says that people in Las Cruces who were concerned about the gentle hermit would look for the light of his campfire at night; when the light didn't appear one evening they went to investigate and found his body.

A relic from an earlier era on the La Cueva Trail in the western foothills of the Organ Mountains

Return the way you came, or continue northwest just a few hundred yards to the Fillmore Canyon Trail, which will bring you to a picnic area. As you walk back to the visitor center, you'll be rewarded with spectacular views of the rugged west face of the Organ Mountains. The mountains were named by early Spanish explorers for their resemblance to the huge pipe organs in Spanish cathedrals. Ask your children what images they might use to describe the mountains.

55. Sitting Bull Falls

Type: Dayhike
Difficulty: Easy
Hikable: Year-round
One way: 1 mile
Starting elevation: 4,660 feet
High point: 5,000 feet
Maps: Lincoln National Forest; Queen 7.5-minute USGS quad
Hazards: Cliffs

As you drive west across the plains from US 285 to the falls, ask your children to note how parched, treeless, and brown the landscape

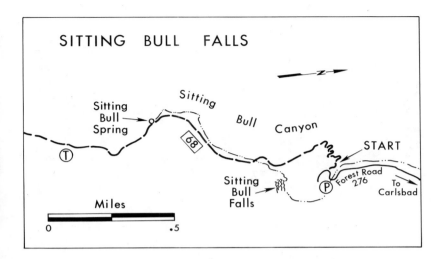

is. That will help them to appreciate the green miracle of Sitting Bull Falls.

Nestled in a canyon in the eastern foothills of the Guadalupe Mountains, Sitting Bull Falls is a perfect side trip for persons visiting Carlsbad Caverns National Park, though a rather long drive is involved and there's no camping at the falls. The falls are reached from Carlsbad by driving about 9 miles northwest on US 285 to NM 137, then driving southwest 24 miles to Forest Road 276; the falls are 7.6 miles away, in a narrow, scenic limestone canyon.

You and your children likely will be interested in the name, Sitting Bull Falls. Could it have anything to do with the famous Sioux chief? Well, lots of "bull" has been spread about the origin of this name. The most widely accepted story involves "Uncle Bill" Jones, a rancher who had come to southeastern New Mexico from Virginia. His brothers had accused him of telling tall tales about his wanderings in the Guadalupes, and when he told them of a waterfall in the arid mountains, they scoffed, "Well, Sitting Bull, if there is a falls there we'll name it after you." There was, and they did.

When you arrive at the site, administered by the Lincoln National Forest, you'll first want to see the falls, which are reached by a concrete walkway just 0.25 mile from the parking area. But when you've sampled the falls and cooled off, take the hike heading up Sitting Bull Canyon above the falls.

Trail 68 begins at the north side of the parking area and ascends 0.25 mile via switchbacks to a shelf. About 0.25 mile farther there's an overlook of the falls (keep children away from the edge).

Sitting Bull Falls, a green miracle (Photo: Lincoln National Forest)

From here the trail follows a relatively level course as it parallels the stream. Numerous very short spurs lead left to a series of emerald pools shaded by large oak trees. Away from the stream the trail passes by such desert plants as sotol, lechuguilla, cat-claw acacia, agave, and several species of yuccas. Ask children to notice how each plant is armed for defense. Indeed, one of the common names for the yucca is Spanish dagger, for its stiff, slender leaves that end in a point as sharp as a dagger's. Ask children also to notice how each plant has evolved to conserve water. Some species, like agaves, have fleshy leaves that can store water, and almost all species have leaf surfaces that are thick and tough so as not to release much moisture into the dry air.

After 0.75 mile from the top of the falls, the stream disappears into the sand and the canyon branches, the trail going left into a narrow, shallow canyon. In the canyon is Sitting Bull Spring, now enclosed in metal and concrete. The trail becomes considerably steeper and rougher here before leveling off after 0.75 mile onto the arid plateau. From the rim there are expansive views of the canyon and beyond.

But the main interest for young hikers is back at the green stream and the wonderful waterfall. On a hot day, its water is irresistible, and for generations the people of southeastern New Mexico have come here to delight in this waterfall in the desert. For many years it was a tradition for families to pack picnic baskets and come here for holidays, especially the Fourth of July, to play in the fall's refreshing mist.

---

56. West Fork of the Gila River

Type: Dayhike or backpack
Difficulty: Moderate to difficult for children
Hikable: June through October
One way: 3 miles
Starting elevation: 5,700 feet
High point: 6,120 feet
Maps: Gila Wilderness (Gila National Forest); Little Turkey Park 7.5-minute USGS quad
Hazards: Seasonally high water

It's ironic that one of New Mexico's most serenely beautiful places has had such a violent history. And ironic, too, that a place that's isolated and relatively unpopulated today was the site of one of the Southwest's most remarkable early civilizations. But even children not interested in history will enjoy the adventure and variety of this hike. And this is one hike where wading not only is permitted but is necessary—be sure to bring old sneakers.

The trailhead for the West Fork of the Gila River is at Gila Cliff Dwellings National Monument, reached from Silver City via NM 15.

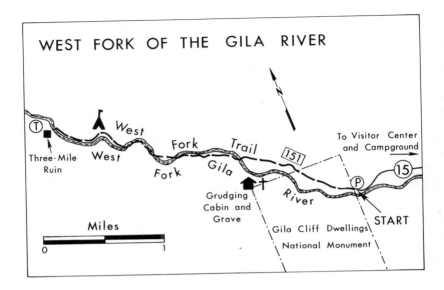

WEST FORK OF THE GILA RIVER

Three-Mile Ruin

West Fork

West Fork Gila Trail

Grudging Cabin and Grave

Gila River

151

To Visitor Center and Campground

15

START

P

Gila Cliff Dwellings National Monument

Miles

0   1

Allow 2 hours to travel the paved but narrow and tortuous road. Two small Gila National Forest campgrounds are near the cliff dwellings, but no other public campsites are available. Current information about conditions in the area are available at the Gila National Forest Visitor Center, about 2 miles before NM 15 ends at the cliff dwellings. About 0.5 mile from the visitor center, on the Middle Fork of the Gila River, is a small hot spring you might be interested in visiting.

Plan to spend a couple of hours the day before your hike visiting the Gila cliff dwellings. In this masonry city, members of the Mogollon culture lived from around A.D. 1000 until their abrupt and mysterious disappearance around 1250. Along the West Fork are numerous reminders of their presence. The ruins are just a short walk from the monument visitor center and parking lot. Children will love climbing ladders to explore the ancient dwellings, where visitors are accompanied by guides. Why did the ancient Indians build here, high in the cliffs? Was it for defense? But from whom? They had departed by the time of the great drought of 1276, but why? Did overpopulation cause their society to collapse? Or internecine conflict? Or some other cause? To these questions archaeologists have no easy answers. Ask your children what they think.

The Gila Cliff Dwellings National Monument is a tiny island in the vast Gila Wilderness. After 1900, concern mounted over loss of animal species and habitat. Among the voices clamoring for conservation was that of Aldo Leopold, later one of America's foremost conservation writers and philosophers, who had been a young forester here with the U.S. Forest Service. In 1924 the U.S. government heeded the warnings and created the Gila Wilderness, the first such wild preserve in the world. The wilderness, named for the river, originally contained 755,000 acres. Later, portions of it were excised to create the Aldo Leopold Wilderness, so the Gila Wilderness now contains 558,065 acres, still the largest in New Mexico.

The West Fork Trail 151, leading into the wilderness, begins at the Gila cliff dwellings parking lot and is marked by a sign. The trail meanders through open forest and meadows on the river's north side before coming after about 1 mile to the first of many river crossings. Because of these crossings, it's wise to inquire about river conditions at the Gila National Forest Visitor Center. Also, you will appreciate walking sticks for extra stability during the crossings.

Just south of this crossing, on a rise on the river's south side, lie the remains of a small log cabin and, about 50 yards up the slope, a grave. Though weathered, the inscription on the headstone can still be read: "William Grudging waylaid and murdered by Tom Wood Oct. 8 1893 age 37 years 8 mos." Local people still discuss the tragic outcome of that old feud.

From here the trail continues to follow the river, crossing it several times as it winds between the canyon's steep walls. After about 2 miles, you'll begin noticing obvious campsites, and you may want to choose one for your party. Though there are no camping restrictions on the West Fork, campers should avoid heavily used sites and adopt a "no trace" ethic. Also, supervise your children if they play near the river.

Three-Mile Ruin—3 miles

The grave of William Grudging, murdered over 100 years ago on the West Fork of the Gila River from the trailhead—is the most popular West Fork destination for hikers. It's a tiny cliff dwelling in a shallow cave on the river's west side. Archaeologists at Gila Cliff Dwellings National Monument say new discoveries still are being made in the Gila backcountry, and the tawny volcanic rock of the canyon is pockmarked with holes and crevices that invite probing. Yet all archaeological sites are very fragile and should not be disturbed; all artifacts, such as pottery fragments, should be admired but not touched.

Wildlife is common here, and you're likely to see white-tailed deer and small mammals such as tassel-eared squirrels, skunks, raccoons, and coyotes. While it's unlikely you'll see one of the region's mountain lions or black bears, their tracks often are found on the river's sandy shore. Grizzly bears are gone from the Gila country, exterminated by relentless hunting that included professional "varmint" hunters such as Ben Lilly, but the other species have outlasted their persecutors.

The plant life here also is interesting—cottonwoods, willows, Virginia creeper, and giant sycamores with buff-colored exfoliating bark reminiscent of the cliffs. Fall is an especially beautiful time along the West Fork, when the foliage is yellow, brown, and crimson.

Because of the abundant wildlife, availability of water, and rich vegetation, the Gila country was beloved by the Apache Indians. From hideouts here they launched raids against European settlers. Until late in the last century, travel in the Gila country was very dangerous, and numerous miners, trappers, and settlers are buried in unmarked graves, the victims of Apache ambushes. Geronimo knew the Gila country well, as did such Apache leaders as Cochise and Mangas Coloradas.

Few children would not delight in exploring the West Fork of the Gila River. And few would not enjoy hearing campfire tales of others who have passed this way—ancient cliff dwellers, Apaches, grizzly bear hunters, archaeologists, even murderers.

Index

About the Author

Bob Julyan was born in Boulder, Colorado, where he grew up hiking the Front Range of the Rocky Mountains. Since that time he has lived in several places, all having some proximity to mountains. He began to write professionally, specializing in geographic history and outdoor recreation, while living in the White Mountains of New Hampshire. Here he and his wife, Mary, wrote *Place Names of the White Mountains* (revised edition, University Press of New England, 1993). His interest in geographic names has also led him to write *Mountain Names* (The Mountaineers, 1984) and *Place Names of New Mexico* (University of New Mexico Press, 1995), a standard reference on the historical place names of the geographic features of the state. He and his wife have lived with their two daughters, Megan and Robin, in New Mexico since 1978. They have traveled throughout the state camping, hiking, telling trail stories, and picking stickers out of socks.

THE MOUNTAINEERS, founded in 1906, is a nonprofit outdoor activity and conservation club, whose mission is "to explore, study, preserve, and enjoy the natural beauty of the outdoors. . . ." Based in Seattle, Washington, the club is now the third-largest such organization in the United States, with 15,000 members and five branches throughout Washington State.

The Mountaineers sponsors both classes and year-round outdoor activities in the Pacific Northwest, which include hiking, mountain climbing, ski-touring, snowshoeing, bicycling, camping, kayaking and canoeing, nature study, sailing, and adventure travel. The club's conservation division supports environmental causes through educational activities, sponsoring legislation, and presenting informational programs. All club activities are led by skilled, experienced volunteers, who are dedicated to promoting safe and responsible enjoyment and preservation of the outdoors.

The Mountaineers Books, an active, nonprofit publishing program of the club, produces guidebooks, instructional texts, historical works, natural history guides, and works on environmental conservation. All books produced by The Mountaineers are aimed at fulfilling the club's mission.

If you would like to participate in these organized outdoor activities or the club's programs, consider a membership in The Mountaineers. For information and an application, write or call The Mountaineers, Club Headquarters, 300 Third Avenue West, Seattle, Washington 98119; (206) 284-6310.

Send or call for our catalog of more than 300 outdoor titles:

 The Mountaineers Books
1001 SW Klickitat Way, Suite 201
Seattle, WA 98134
1-800-553-4453